COMPREHENSION
STRATEGY
ASSESSMENT

Grade 3

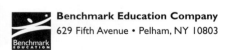

Benchmark Education Company
629 Fifth Avenue • Pelham, NY 10803

Printed in Guangzhou, China. 4401/0613/CA21301023

ISBN: 978-1-4108-5054-6
For ordering information, call Toll-Free 1-877-236-2465 or visit our Web site at www.benchmarkeducation.com.

Table of Contents

Introduction

Comprehension Strategy Assessment provides assessments for measuring students' grasp of comprehension strategies in both reading and listening. Information from these assessments can be used to support instruction.

This book contains three types of assessments:

- The **Pretest** is designed to assess students' reading comprehension strategies at the beginning of the school year. It contains a series of seven reading passages, both fiction and nonfiction, with a total of thirty-two multiple-choice items. Information from the Pretest can be used to help plan instruction, make curriculum decisions, and select reading materials to match students' needs. Pretest scores can also be used as baseline data for evaluating students' progress from the beginning of the school year to the end.

- **Ongoing Comprehension Strategy Assessments** are focused, two-page assessments to be administered periodically during the school year. Each assessment includes a reading passage and a set of five test items to measure one specific strategy. There are two assessments per strategy, and they are intended to be used to monitor students' progress. They may be administered after completing instruction in particular strategies, or they may be administered at other appropriate times, such as at the end of each grading period. These pages may be used as reading assessments or listening assessments.

- The **Posttest** is parallel to the Pretest. It contains the same number of reading passages and items as the Pretest, and it tests the same strategies. The Posttest is designed to be administered at the end of the school year as a final evaluation of students' progress in comparison to their performance at the beginning of the year.

The next few pages in this book provide directions for administering and scoring the assessments and using the assessment results. Answer keys for all of the assessments can be found at the beginning of each section. Scoring Charts for scoring the assessments and recording results can be found on pages 131–133.

DIRECTIONS FOR ADMINISTERING AND SCORING ASSESSMENTS

All of the assessments in this book may be administered to students individually or in a group. We recommend administering the Pretest and Posttest to all students at the same time. The Ongoing Comprehension Strategy Assessments may be administered in the same way, or they may be administered individually or in small groups to different students at different times. Detailed guidelines for administering and scoring each type of assessment are presented below.

GUIDELINES FOR USING THE PRETEST

The Pretest is fourteen pages long. It includes seven one-page reading passages and a set of multiple-choice questions for each passage: thirty-two items total. These thirty-two items measure eight "clusters" of strategies and skills (as listed on the Scoring Chart, page 131) with four items per cluster. Each cluster has two to four strategies grouped by similarities. For example, "Identify Main Idea" and "Summarize or Paraphrase Information" are grouped together in one cluster because they involve similar thinking skills (distinguishing essential from inessential information). Each cluster has been labeled with a title that reflects the key thinking skill, such as "Distinguishing Important Information."

Plan for about an hour to administer the Pretest, but allow more time if needed. Students should be allowed to finish answering every question. Depending on the students and your situation, you may want to administer the Pretest in two parts in different sittings.

To Administer the Pretest:

1. Make a copy of the test for each student.

2. Tell students to write their names and the date at the top of each test page.

3. Read the directions on the first page and make sure students understand what to do.

4. Instruct students to read each passage and answer the questions that go with it.

5. For each multiple-choice question, instruct students to choose the best answer and fill in the bubble beside the answer they choose.

6. Option: If you prefer, you may copy the answer sheet on page 130 of this book and instruct students to fill in the answers on the answer sheet.

7. When students have finished, collect the tests.

To Score the Pretest:

1. Make a copy of the Individual Pretest/Posttest Scoring Chart (see page 131) for each student.

2. Refer to the Pretest Answer Key on page 13. The Answer Key gives the letter of the correct response to each question.

3. Mark each question correct or incorrect on the test page (or on the answer sheet).

4. To find the total test score, count the number of items answered correctly.

5. To score by cluster, use the Individual Pretest/Posttest Scoring Chart. Circle the number of each item answered correctly. The item numbers are organized by clusters of tested skills.

6. For each cluster on the scoring chart, add the number of items answered correctly (for example, three of four). Write the number correct in the right-hand column under Pretest Score.

Using the Results:

1. Use the results of the Pretest to determine each student's current level of reading ability, as well as his or her proficiencies in the strategies being tested.

2. As explained earlier, the items in the Pretest measure strategies in particular clusters. A student's score on a particular cluster can pinpoint specific instructional needs. A student who answers correctly fewer than 3 of the 4 items in each cluster may need focused instructional attention on those particular strategies.

3. Plotting scores on the Individual and Group Pretest/Posttest Scoring Charts provides a handy reference for monitoring students' growth and development. Such information can be used to identify the skills and strategies to be reinforced for a whole group, small group, or individual.

4. Store the Pretest/Posttest Scoring Charts in an appropriate location for referral during the school year and for end-of-year comparison of Pretest and Posttest scores.

GUIDELINES FOR USING THE ONGOING COMPREHENSION STRATEGY ASSESSMENTS

In this program, Grade 3 covers nineteen comprehension and word solving strategies. In this book you will find two assessments for each strategy (arranged in alphabetical order by strategy within Comprehension Skills and Word Solving Skills). The assessments are numbered 1 through 38, and each assessment is two pages long.

The purpose of these assessments is to determine how well students have learned each strategy. You may want to administer the two strategy-based assessments at set times of the year (such as during the second and third quarters), or you can administer an assessment for a specific strategy just after teaching the strategy in the classroom. Although the assessments are numbered sequentially 1 through 38, they do not need to be administered in any set order. You may choose to assess any strategy in whatever order you teach them.

Each Ongoing Comprehension Strategy Assessment comprises a one-page reading passage and a set of five questions. For comprehension and vocabulary strategies, three of the items are multiple choice questions; the other two are short-answer questions that require students to write their own answers. Most of these responses will be one to three sentences long. For assessments of word solving skills, all five items are multiple choice.

Plan for fifteen to twenty minutes to administer an Ongoing Comprehension Strategy Assessment, but allow more time if needed.

To Administer an Ongoing Assessment:

1. Make a copy of the assessment for each student.

2. Tell students to write their name and the date at the top of each test page.

3. Direct students to read each passage and answer the questions that go with it.

4. For each multiple-choice question, instruct students to choose the best answer and fill in the bubble beside the answer they choose.

5. For short-answer questions, instruct students to write their responses (in phrases or complete sentences) on the lines provided.

Listening Comprehension

Ongoing Assessments 1 through 32 are intended primarily for use as written assessments of reading comprehension. However, they may also be used as measures of listening comprehension. To use the Ongoing Assessments for listening purposes, read the passage aloud to the student(s) and direct the student(s) to answer the questions. Students may respond by marking and writing their answers on the test page, or you may instruct students to give oral responses. If preferred, you may use one of the two Ongoing Assessments for reading comprehension and the other for listening comprehension.

To Score the Ongoing Assessment:

6. Refer to the appropriate Answer Key (on pages 30–37). The Answer Key gives the letter of the correct response for each multiple-choice question. It gives a sample correct response for each short-answer question.

7. Mark each question correct or incorrect on the test page. You may need to interpret the student's written responses and decide whether they are correct or incorrect, based on the sample answers in the Answer Key.

8. To find the total score, count the number of items answered correctly.

Using the Results:

9. Use the results of the Ongoing Assessment to evaluate each student's understanding of the tested strategy or skill.

10. A student who understands and applies a given strategy should answer at least four of the five items correctly. A student who answers correctly fewer than four items may need additional instruction on a particular strategy.

11. Use the Ongoing Strategy Assessment Record to keep track of a student's scores on the assessments during the school year. The record provides space for writing the score on each of the two strategy assessments and for noting comments relevant to a student's progress in learning a particular strategy.

GUIDELINES FOR USING THE POSTTEST

The Posttest contains the same number of reading passages and items as the Pretest and should be administered and scored in the same way. The test items on the Posttest measure the same skills as the Pretest and are in the same order. Thus, the item numbers on the Individual Pretest/Posttest Scoring Chart are the same for both tests.

Use the results of the Posttest to determine each student's current level of reading ability, as well as his or her proficiencies in the strategies being tested. Compare the student's scores on the Pretest and Posttest—and on each strategy cluster within the tests—to evaluate the student's progress since the beginning of the year.

Answer Key

1. B	17. C
2. C	18. B
3. D	19. D
4. A	20. A
5. D	21. C
6. D	22. A
7. C	23. B
8. A	24. A
9. B	25. C
10. C	26. C
11. A	27. A
12. B	28. B
13. D	29. D
14. B	30. C
15. A	31. B
16. D	32. D

Pretest Answer Key

Name _____ Date _____

Directions: Read the passage. Then use the information from the passage to answer questions 1–4.

The Dog and the Wolf

Long ago, a shopkeeper lived in a village. He got a dog to keep watch over his shop. The dog did a fine job for a few years and then grew old. The shopkeeper chased the dog from the village.

The dog wandered for days in the woods with nothing to eat. It grew <u>weak</u> and lay down to rest. Just then, a wolf jumped on the dog and snarled, "You are my next meal!"

"What a poor meal that will be," replied the dog. "Why don't you feed me for a few days and fatten me up? Then I will be a real feast for you."

For the next three days, the dog rested and ate the food it got from the wolf. By the third day, the dog felt rested and strong.

On the fourth day, the wolf jumped on the dog again. "Now I shall eat you!" it snarled.

But the dog easily tossed the wolf off and pinned it down. The wolf was surprised and helpless. "What are you going to do with me?" the wolf asked the dog.

"Nothing at all," said the dog, as it released the wolf. "You helped me get strong again. Now I will thank you by sparing your life."

Name _____ Date _____

1. Which words best describe the character of the dog in this story?

Ⓐ quiet and proud

Ⓑ clever and kind

Ⓒ angry and foolish

Ⓓ mean and sly

2. What did the shopkeeper do in this story?

Ⓐ He taught the dog to hunt.

Ⓑ He saved the dog from the wolf.

Ⓒ He chased the dog away.

Ⓓ He took care of the dog when it was old.

3. Which detail from this story could NOT really happen?

Ⓐ The dog kept watch over a shop.

Ⓑ The dog wandered for days in the woods.

Ⓒ The wolf jumped on the dog.

Ⓓ The wolf snarled, "You are my next meal!"

4. The story says that the dog grew <u>weak</u>. Which word from the story means about the same as <u>weak</u>?

Ⓐ helpless

Ⓑ strong

Ⓒ surprised

Ⓓ fine

Name _____ Date _____

Directions: Read the passage. Then use the information from the passage to answer questions 5–8.

When Money Grew on Trees

Many Americans moved west in the 1800s. Some wanted to start over in a new place. Some wanted land for farming. Others hoped to get rich. Most people thought finding gold was a sure way to get rich. A man named Henderson Luelling had his own idea. He moved west with something to plant. It grew into a fortune.

In 1846, Luelling decided to move his family from Iowa to Oregon. He bought three wagons for the trip. Only one was for his family's things. He packed the other two wagons with fruit trees.

The wagons were a funny sight on the trail. Luelling worked hard to keep the trees alive. His daughter Eliza <u>resented</u> the fuss he made about the trees. She wanted him to take more interest in her.

When the family reached Oregon, Luelling planted the trees. Before long, Luelling was selling fruit. Thanks to his clever idea and hard work, Luelling became a rich man.

5. What is the main idea of this passage?

Ⓐ Many Americans moved west in the 1800s.

Ⓑ Some people moved west to start over in a new place.

Ⓒ Many people who moved west thought finding gold was the best way to get rich.

Ⓓ Henderson Luelling made a fortune when he moved west and planted fruit trees.

6. Which detail shows that Luelling's idea made him rich?

Ⓐ Luelling bought three wagons, but only one was for his family.

Ⓑ The tree-filled wagons were a funny sight.

Ⓒ Luelling's daughter wanted him to show more interest in her.

Ⓓ Before long, Luelling was selling fruit.

7. The passage says, "His daughter Eliza <u>resented</u> the fuss he made about the trees." What does <u>resented</u> mean?

Ⓐ remembered

Ⓑ noticed

Ⓒ disliked

Ⓓ helped

8. The author wrote this passage to _____.

Ⓐ tell the story of Henderson Luelling and his trees

Ⓑ describe ways for people to get rich

Ⓒ show how easy it is to grow fruit trees

Ⓓ explain why Americans move from one place to another

Name _____ Date _____

Directions: Read the passage. Then use the information from the passage to answer questions 9–12.

Basketball Blues

Ross walked in the door and sank into a chair. Then he let out a long sigh. Grandma knew what that meant.

"What's wrong?" she asked.

"We played basketball in gym today," answered Ross, "and I was the worst player in the whole class."

Grandma poured a glass of chocolate milk. She brought it to Ross and said, "Well, at least it's over. Try to forget about it."

"I can't," said Ross. "Ms. Howe says we'll be playing basketball for four weeks. That's four more weeks of <u>misery</u>."

Thump . . . thump . . . thump . . . The sound was coming from outside. Grandma and Ross looked out the window and saw Brianna next door, bouncing a basketball. As they watched, Brianna spun to face a hoop over the garage door. Then she took a shot. The ball dropped through the net.

Grandma whistled and said, "Looks like Brianna's a good player."

Ross nodded glumly. "She scored lots of points in gym today. I don't know how she does it."

"Well, I do!" Grandma laughed. "While you're in here feeling sorry for yourself, Brianna's out there practicing." Then Grandma added, "You can settle for being the worst player in class, Ross, or you can do something about it. It's up to you."

Thump . . . thump . . . thump . . . Ross sat thinking for a minute. Then he walked out the door and headed for Brianna's yard.

9. What will probably happen next?

Ⓐ Ross will invite Brianna to his house.

Ⓑ Brianna and Ross will practice basketball together.

Ⓒ Grandma will give Ross some basketball tips.

Ⓓ Ross will stop playing basketball.

10. What is Ross's problem in this story?

Ⓐ His grandmother does not understand him.

Ⓑ He does not get along with Brianna.

Ⓒ He is not a very good basketball player.

Ⓓ He does not like his gym teacher.

11. What can you tell about Brianna from this story?

Ⓐ She spends a lot of time practicing basketball.

Ⓑ She is good at many different sports.

Ⓒ She feels sorry for Ross.

Ⓓ She is a show-off in gym class.

12. In the story, Ross says, "That's four more weeks of <u>misery</u>." What does <u>misery</u> mean?

Ⓐ hard work

Ⓑ unhappiness

Ⓒ confusion

Ⓓ excitement

Name _____ Date _____

Directions: Read the passage. Then use the information from the passage to answer questions 13–17.

A Kid Who Never Grew Up

Shel Silverstein was a great writer. For more than 30 years, he wrote plays, stories, poems, and songs. People of all ages love Silverstein's work. But he is best known for his children's books.

Shel Silverstein was born in Chicago in 1932. He started drawing and writing when he was a teenager. Later he joined the army. There he drew cartoons for the magazine *Stars and Stripes*. It was the perfect job for Shel.

After Silverstein left the army, he didn't know what to do. He loved writing and illustrating. But he didn't think he could make money doing these things. A friend thought he could. He <u>coaxed</u> Shel into writing and illustrating children's stories. Silverstein's first book was a small hit. His second book was *The Giving Tree*. It told about a tree that gave its fruit and branches to a boy, just to make him happy. The story was sweet and sad. It was also a big hit.

In his next book, Shel Silverstein went from sweet to funny. *Where the Sidewalk Ends* came out in 1974. It includes more than 100 poems and drawings that make kids laugh out loud. It's hard to believe anyone could write so many silly poems. But Silverstein was just getting started. *A Light in the Attic* came out in 1981. *Falling Up* followed in 1996. These books of poems and drawings were just as funny as the first one.

Shel Silverstein died in 1999. He was 68 years old. But in a way, Silverstein was a kid who never grew up. He was a very funny kid, too, who shared some great jokes with the world.

20 **Comprehension Strategy Assessment • Grade 3**

13. **Most of the information in this passage is organized by _____.**
Ⓐ cause and effect   Ⓑ problem and solution
Ⓒ compare and contrast   Ⓓ time order

14. **Why was drawing cartoons for *Stars and Stripes* a good job for Silverstein?**
Ⓐ He got paid a lot of money.
Ⓑ He liked to draw and write.
Ⓒ He became very famous.
Ⓓ He did not want to work hard.

15. **Which sentence from the passage states an opinion?**
Ⓐ Shel Silverstein was a great writer.
Ⓑ Shel Silverstein was born in Chicago in 1932.
Ⓒ He started drawing and writing when he was a teenager.
Ⓓ *Where the Sidewalk Ends* came out in 1974.

16. **The passage says, "He <u>coaxed</u> Shel into writing and illustrating children's stories." What does <u>coaxed</u> mean?**
Ⓐ forced   Ⓑ paid
Ⓒ asked   Ⓓ persuaded

17. **The author wrote this passage to _____.**
Ⓐ explain how Shel Silverstein drew his cartoons
Ⓑ teach people how to write poems
Ⓒ tell about Shel Silverstein and his children's books
Ⓓ convince readers to buy children's books

Name_____ Date _____

Directions: Read the passage. Then use the information from the passage to answer questions 18–22.

How Old Is Old?

In the United States, the average person lives to be 77 years old. But many people live to be 90 or older. In fact, the oldest known person reached the <u>remarkable</u> age of 122!

Many animals have much shorter lives than people. Most horses live to about 20. Lobsters live about 15 years. A few animals live much longer than people. Some turtles live 100 years or more. A fish called a sturgeon can live to be 150.

Time Flies for the Mayfly!

The tiny mayfly has a very short life. Most adult mayflies live for only a few hours—just long enough to find a mate.

You can find out how long some other animals live by looking at the graph.

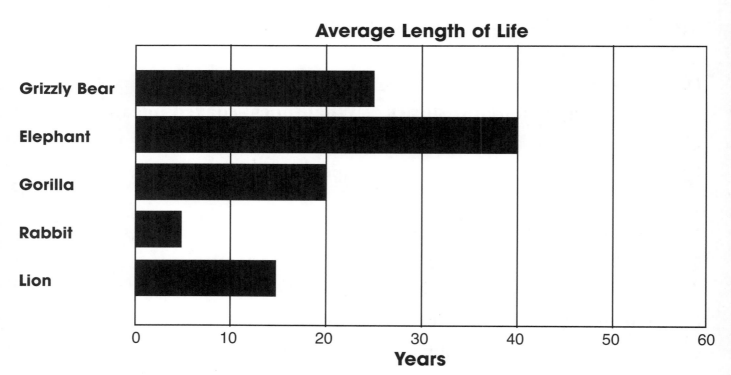

Average Length of Life

Animal	Years
Grizzly Bear	25
Elephant	40
Gorilla	20
Rabbit	5
Lion	15

Years (0, 10, 20, 30, 40, 50, 60)

18. The passage says, "The oldest known person reached the remarkable age of 122!" What does remarkable mean?

Ⓐ fine   Ⓑ amazing

Ⓒ scary   Ⓓ gentle

19. Which is the best summary of the first two paragraphs?

Ⓐ People live much longer than horses, lobsters, and chickens.

Ⓑ Horses live longer than lobsters and chickens. A sturgeon lives longer than a turtle.

Ⓒ People don't live as long as sturgeons or turtles.

Ⓓ Many animals don't live as long as people. But a few animals live much longer.

20. How long do most mayflies live?

Ⓐ a few hours   Ⓑ a week or two

Ⓒ about a year   Ⓓ three or four years

21. Which of these animals lives the longest?

Ⓐ lion   Ⓑ gorilla

Ⓒ elephant   Ⓓ grizzly bear

22. About how long does a rabbit live?

Ⓐ 5 years   Ⓑ 15 years

Ⓒ 20 years   Ⓓ 25 years

Name _____ Date _____

Directions: Read the passage. Then use the information from the passage to answer questions 23–27.

Yoshi's Journal

May 12

Today I went to Spencer's house. We built a little wooden boat and took it to the creek. The boat sailed great until it got stuck on a log. Spencer and I had to wade in to <u>retrieve</u> it. We got wet and muddy, but we had a blast!

May 15

I went to Will's house after school. We played a car racing game on his computer. At first Will kept beating me. But then he showed me the trick to getting a really high score. I had so much fun I didn't want to go home.

May 17

Tomorrow Will and Spencer are coming to my house after school. They are my two best friends in the whole third grade. Spencer's going to bring his boat, and Will's going to bring his computer game. I can't wait!

May 18

Will and Spencer just went home. What a relief! No one had much fun. First we went to the creek, but Will just complained the whole time. "Who wants to get dirty floating a dumb toy boat?" he kept saying.

Then we went back to the house. Will and I played on the computer, but Spencer refused. He got mad at Will and me. Finally Mom told us to find something everyone wanted to do. So we watched cartoons until Spencer and Will left. We were all really bored, but at least we weren't arguing.

23. How does Yoshi probably feel about what happened when his friends came to his house?

Ⓐ He can't wait to have them over again.

Ⓑ He is sorry everyone had trouble getting along.

Ⓒ He feels angry that his mother told them what to do.

Ⓓ He is glad everyone likes watching TV.

24. How are Spencer and Will alike?

Ⓐ Both are friends of Yoshi.

Ⓑ Both like getting wet and muddy.

Ⓒ Both are good at computer games.

Ⓓ Both have toy boats.

25. What happened next after Yoshi played at Spencer's house?

Ⓐ Spencer played at Yoshi's house.

Ⓑ Spencer and Will became friends.

Ⓒ Yoshi played at Will's house.

Ⓓ Spencer got mad at Will and Yoshi.

26. The boys stopped arguing once they decided to _____.

Ⓐ build a toy boat   Ⓑ play at the creek

Ⓒ watch cartoons   Ⓓ play computer games

27. The passage says, "Spencer and I had to wade in to <u>retrieve</u> it." What does <u>retrieve</u> mean?

Ⓐ get back again   Ⓑ lose

Ⓒ take apart   Ⓓ watch

Name _____ Date _____

Directions: Read the passage. Then use the information from the passage to answer questions 28–32.

Get Some Sleep!

Sleep is something everyone needs. Sleep gives your body and brain a chance to rest. What happens when you don't get enough sleep? You have trouble thinking clearly or acting quickly. You make mistakes. You get pretty grumpy, too. When you're very <u>tired</u>, your mind can <u>deceive</u> you. You may "see" or "hear" things that aren't real. But these problems go away once you are rested. There really is nothing better than a good night's sleep.

Sleep is important for many other animals, too. All mammals need to sleep. So do reptiles and birds. But insects and fish are different. They may become quiet and still for a while, but they don't really fall asleep the way you do.

When you are in a deep sleep, you dream. A dream may last from 5 to 30 minutes. You probably dream every night, but you forget most of your dreams. If something wakes you up in the middle of a dream, you will remember it.

Do animals that sleep also dream? Some do, and some don't. Birds dream a little bit, but reptiles don't dream at all. All mammals, including dogs and cats, dream while they sleep. So when you say good night to your pet, you might add, "Sweet dreams!"

28. How are fish and insects different from other animals?
- Ⓐ They sleep more.
- Ⓑ They rest without sleeping.
- Ⓒ They are less active.
- Ⓓ They sleep without dreaming.

29. Which sentence from the passage states an opinion?
- Ⓐ Sleep gives your body and brain a chance to rest.
- Ⓑ A dream may last from 5 to 30 minutes.
- Ⓒ But these problems go away once you are rested.
- Ⓓ There really is nothing better than a good night's sleep.

30. The passage says, "When you're very tired, your mind can deceive you." What does deceive mean?
- Ⓐ accept or take
- Ⓑ go back again
- Ⓒ trick or fool
- Ⓓ make better

31. Sometimes people get tired. Which word from the passage means the opposite of tired?
- Ⓐ clearly
- Ⓑ rested
- Ⓒ quiet
- Ⓓ grumpy

32. Which is the best summary of the last paragraph?
- Ⓐ Some animals dream when they sleep. Cats and dogs do. So do mammals and birds.
- Ⓑ Reptiles don't dream. But some mammals, like cats and dogs, have dreams.
- Ⓒ Cats and dogs are mammals. They dream when they sleep.
- Ⓓ Mammals and birds dream when they sleep. But reptiles sleep without dreaming.

STOP
END OF PRETEST

Assessments

Ongoing Comprehension Strategy Assessments

Assessment 1: First on the Courts
(Analyze Character)
1. D
2. A
3. C
4. Examples: After quitting school, she later went back to get her diploma. Or, she kept practicing hard to become a better tennis player.
5. Possible answers: Yes, Althea Gibson was a sports legend. She worked hard and was very determined. She overcame hardship to become a winner. Her courage helped those who came after her.

Assessment 2: The Contest
(Analyze Character)
1. B
2. C
3. D
4. Example: She will not mind because she is more interested in the quarters and the states than in winning the contest.
5. Possible responses: She is a neat and careful worker. She looks at everything carefully and likes to learn about things. She has good ideas, such as looking for coins in the car.

Assessment 3: Buried Alive
(Analyze Story Elements)
1. D
2. C
3. B
4. The dog identified where the skier was buried.
5. Example: Rescuers dug him out of the snow and strapped him into a sled. Then they took him down the mountain.

Assessment 4: A Long Week
(Analyze Story Elements)
1. A
2. C
3. B
4. Examples: Mama does not smile. She does not eat. She is very hot. She does not hear anything. She has been asleep for six days.
5. Possible response: Rebecca will ride her pony to town and bring back the doctor. Papa will stay home and take care of Mama.

Assessment 5: The Channel Tunnel

(Analyze Text Structure and Organization)

1. A
2. C
3. B
4. Examples: They worked together and shared the costs. They started digging from each end and met in the middle.
5. People could now take their cars from England to France and back.

Assessment 6: Comics Then and Now

(Analyze Text Structure and Organization)

1. C
2. D
3. A
4. Example: You can find out from the fourth paragraph, which tells of the first comic book about a superhero.
5. Example: The title shows that the subject is comics. The words then and now suggest that the passage tells how comics have changed.

Assessment 7: Leonardo da Vinci: Master of Invention

(Compare and Contrast)

1. B
2. D
3. B
4. It was used to move air.
5. Example: An airplane and the flying ship both fly through the air, have wings, and carry people.

Assessment 8: A Different Kind of Ride

(Compare and Contrast)

1. A
2. C
3. D
4. Example: Most people ride near home in warm weather, but Doug rides on ice and snow in Antarctica.
5. Example: Doug's bike has very fat tires, it has no plastic parts, it costs more money, and it only works well on ice and snow.

Assessment 9: The Most Exciting Job in the World

(Distinguish Fact from Opinion)

1. B
2. B
3. C
4. Examples of facts: The probe worked for hours. Scientists are studying information from the probe. It will take many years to study the information. Example of an opinion: It was very exciting.
5. Example: A good scientist must like to learn new things, be curious, and be patient.

Assessment 10: New Video Fun from Giant Games

(Distinguish Fact from Opinion)

1. D
2. B
3. D
4. Example: "Build-A-World and Build-A-Team cost $30.00 each." This is a fact because it can be verified.
5. Example: "Build-A-Team is a ton of fun!" This is an opinion because it expresses a personal feeling and cannot be verified from the text.

Assessment 11: Big Bad Wolf's Bad Hair Day

(Distinguish Real from Make-Believe)

1. C
2. B
3. A
4. Example: Little Red Riding Hood runs into a cottage.
5. Example: It tells about a wolf that talks, wears a dress and bonnet, and sits in a hair salon reading a magazine.

Assessment 12: Grandfather Bear's Promise

(Distinguish Real from Make-Believe)

1. A
2. C
3. C
4. Examples: The animals talk. The fox sings and skips.
5. Possible answers: A bear cannot make or keep a promise. Even if Grandfather Bear lost his tail, other bears would still have their tails.

Assessment 13: Growing Up Shawnee

(Draw Conclusions)

1. B
2. D
3. C
4. Example: They had to learn different things. The boys spent their time hunting, while the girls prepared food and made clothing.
5. Example: "They learned to tan animal hides and make pots out of clay".

Assessment 14: Trains of the Future?

(Draw Conclusions)

1. A
2. C
3. C
4. Examples: Maglev trains are expensive. Some people think they are not very practical.
5. Example: Power from the electromagnets lifts the train so it does not actually run on the track.

Assessment 15: A Sweet Time of Year

(Evaluate Author's Purpose and Point of View)

1. A
2. B
3. D
4. Example: The author thinks it is a great time of year. He says, "Making syrup is fun" and "Syrup makers love this time of year."
5. Example: The author loves maple syrup. "It smells wonderful, and it tastes great."

Assessment 16: From the Police Chief's Mailbag

(Evaluate Author's Purpose and Point of View)

1. C
2. A
3. B
4. Example: She wants the chief to call and say he will help.
5. Examples: She thinks children should be able to ride. She thinks it is fun. She thinks it is not safe without a crossing guard.

Assessment 17: The Tundra

(Identify Cause and Effect)

1. B
2. A
3. D
4. Reasons: People are driving snowmobiles and cars into the area, and people are hunting the animals.
5. Example: Plants die, animals lack food, and the number of animals gets smaller.

Assessment 18: Helping Some Big Babies

(Identify Cause and Effect)

1. B
2. C
3. B
4. Reasons: Farmers kill elephants that get on their farms. Hunters kill elephants to get ivory.
5. Possible answers: No one would buy ivory. Hunters could not sell ivory. No one would hunt elephants. There would be fewer orphan elephants.

Assessment 19: The Great Pyramid

(Identify Main Idea and Supporting Details)

1. A
2. C
3. B
4. Early visitors stole nearly everything from the Great Pyramid.
5. Possible answers: King Khufu lived around 2,500 B.C. He had the Great Pyramid built. He ruled for about 20 years. He may have been a bad ruler who forced his people to build the pyramid.

Assessment 20: Become a Cloud Watcher

(Identify Main Idea and Supporting Details)

1. A
2. C
3. D
4. Examples: They bring bad weather. They bring rain or hail. They may bring thunder and lightning. They may bring tornadoes.
5. Answers will vary. Examples: "Clouds and Weather," "Watching the Clouds."

Assessment 21: Making a Budget

(Identify Sequence or Steps in a Process)

1. C
2. D
3. B
4. Example: Write all necessary expenses, or money you must spend.
5. Example: Figure out how much money came in and how much you spent. Then fill in the boxes on the chart under "What Really Happened."

Assessment 22: All Mixed Up

(Identify Sequence or Steps in a Process)

1. C
2. D
3. A
4. Example: The water particles move around, and the food-coloring particles blend together.
5. Possible answer: Dispose of the orange water, clean the jar, and clean up the area where you did the experiment.

Assessment 23: Just Not Herself

(Make Inferences)

1. B
2. D
3. A
4. Hank's phone number and a picture of Snowshoes
5. Hank named her Snowshoes because she had white paws.

Assessment 24: Harriet the Tortoise

(Make Inferences)

1. A
2. D
3. B
4. Possible answers: Harriet lives in comfort. She is fed a healthful diet of plants.
5. Examples: She is old and might suffer from being ridden; The zookeepers want to take care of her and keep her safe.

Assessment 25: She Says, He Says

(Make Predictions)

1. C
2. A
3. D
4. He will bring his sand toys.
5. Example: Each of them will find out that the other can't swim well.

Assessment 26: Giving Robots a Sense of Touch

(Make Predictions)

1. B
2. C
3. D
4. Example: It will be able to sense or feel heat, pressure, and movement through its skin.
5. Possible answer: Robots will do repetitive, boring jobs that people have trouble doing, such as assembly line work in a factory or packing boxes in a plant.

Assessment 27: A Look at Lakes

(Summarize or Paraphrase Information)

1. D
2. A
3. C
4. Example: Saltwater lakes are found in hot, dry climates. Evaporation of water causes salt to build up in these lakes.
5. Example: A lake may dry up from a hot climate. The water in the lake evaporates faster than water flows in.

Assessment 28: Measuring Time

(Summarize or Paraphrase Information)

1. A
2. C
3. D
4. Possible answer: The first ways to measure time were sticks and sundials that used the sun. These were used for 3,000 years. Then, starting around A.D. 900, candle clocks measured time as they burned down. Sandglasses measured time as sand passed through them.
5. Example: Early clocks were big and inaccurate. Springs allowed them to be smaller and more precise. Since the 1920s, most clocks have been made with quartz crystals.

Assessment 29: Circus Smirkus

(Use Graphic Features to Interpret Information)

1. A
2. C
3. D
4. The Smirkus School of Circus Arts opened in Essex, VT.
5. Example: The Big Top Tour is a traveling circus group. It goes to 15 towns and gives 72 shows during the summer.

Assessment 30: Homemade Homes

(Use Graphic Features to Interpret Information)

1. B
2. C
3. B
4. Examples: They are both round; both are more or less dome-shaped; both have flexible or removable walls.
5. Examples: Most homes in the United States are rectangular with peaked or sloped roofs; most are built with factory materials; most are permanent, not moveable.

Assessment 31: Traveling Plants

(Use Text Features to Locate Information)

1. C
2. A
3. C
4. Example: When the jelly case floats away, the jelly melts and the seeds are released.
5. Plantain, burdock, and Queen Anne's lace

Assessment 32: Use Your Beach Treasures

(Use Text Features to Locate Information)

1. C
2. B
3. D
4. a kind of light or lamp
5. Examples: With sand you can make a lantern; you can make a picture with pebbles; you can make chimes with shells or an ornament with beach glass.

Assessment 33: She Put Science Into Words

(Identify Synonyms, Antonyms, and Homonyms)

1. B
2. B
3. C
4. A
5. D

Assessment 34: Today's Rodeo
(Identify Synonyms, Antonyms, and Homonyms)
1. D
2. C
3. A
4. D
5. B

Assessment 35: Crickets
(Use Context Clues to Determine Word Meaning)
1. D
2. A
3. A
4. Examples: hop toward; travel quickly
5. Examples: count the number; add 40

Assessment 36: Crossing the Country
(Use Context Clues to Determine Word Meaning)
1. C
2. C
3. B
4. Examples: He packed his car. He left California.
5. Example: They had traveled all over. Now they were going home.

Assessment 37: Everyday Inventions
(Use Knowledge of Word Structure to Determine Word Meaning)
1. C
2. A
3. D
4. B
5. C

Assessment 38: The Little Giant
(Use Knowledge of Word Structure to Determine Word Meaning)
1. C
2. A
3. D
4. B
5. D

Name _____ Date _____

Directions: Read the passage. Then use the information from the passage to answer questions 1–5.

First on the Courts

Althea Gibson played many sports when she was young. Then someone taught her to play tennis. She knew it was the sport for her. She quit school to play tennis full time.

Gibson played in a black women's tennis league. She won many games. During this time, she also went back to school. She got her high school diploma.

In 1950, Gibson became the first African American woman to play in the U.S. Nationals. She lost the first set and won the second set. In the third set, she lost again. But she decided to keep trying.

Many tennis clubs did not let Gibson play because she was African American. Some hotels would not give her a room. But Gibson did not let this get her down. She kept playing hard. She wanted to be the best. Soon she started to win both singles and doubles matches. At the U.S. Nationals in 1956, though, she lost again.

The next year, Gibson's hard work paid off. She won the U.S. Nationals. She was named Female Athlete of the Year. She was the first African American to win that honor.

Althea Gibson's success made it easier for other African Americans, and other women, to succeed in sports. One great female tennis player was Billie Jean King. She said that many other women would have had a much harder time if not for Gibson. Althea Gibson showed them it could be done.

Name _____ Date_____

1. **Althea Gibson won the U.S. Nationals after many tries. What does that tell you about her character?**
   - Ⓐ She did not like attention.
   - Ⓑ She was very shy.
   - Ⓒ She was very smart.
   - Ⓓ She was very determined.

2. **Which detail shows that Althea Gibson faced hardship with bravery?**
   - Ⓐ She kept playing even though clubs and hotels would not let her in.
   - Ⓑ She went back to school and got her diploma.
   - Ⓒ She played both singles and doubles matches.
   - Ⓓ She was named Female Athlete of the Year.

3. **What do Billie Jean King's words tell you about Gibson?**
   - Ⓐ She was scared but overcame her fear.
   - Ⓑ She was very lucky to have done as well as she did.
   - Ⓒ She eased the way for other women in sports.
   - Ⓓ She was unhappy most of the time.

4. **How can you tell that Althea Gibson always wanted to improve herself? Give one detail from the passage to support this idea.**

   _____

   _____

5. **Do you think Althea Gibson is a sports legend? Use information about her character to support your answer.**

   _____

   _____

Name _____ Date _____

Directions: Read the passage. Then use the information from the passage to answer questions 1–5.

The Contest

Jessie paid for her lunch. She took her change and put it on her tray. Then she sat down to eat with her friends.

"Look at your quarter!" Jon said. "There's a horse on it! This is so cool!"

Jessie looked closely at the quarter. It was true! On one side there was a picture of George Washington, and on the other side was a horse. Above the horse was the word *Kentucky*.

After lunch, Jessie and Jon showed the quarter to Mr. Cho. "This is a state quarter," he told them. "The first state quarters were made in 1999. Soon there will be a special quarter for every state."

"Let's have a contest!" Jon said to Jessie. "Let's see who can find more state quarters, but each one has to be different."

That night, Jessie looked at the coins in her bank. She asked Dad to check the coins in his pockets. She even looked in the little coin cup in the car. All together she found seven different quarters. Jessie studied each one. They were so interesting! Each one showed something important about the state. Jessie got some paper and made a neat list of the seven states. Then she drew a picture of each quarter.

Jon told his family about the contest. "Let's all look for quarters!" he said. Jon's family all jumped up to look. Jon found three quarters, and his mother and father gave him ten more. His brother gave him five, and his sister gave him one. Jon counted all the quarters. "I have 19 quarters, and there are 13 different ones! I'll win the contest for sure," he said.

Name _____ Date_____

1. What detail from the passage tells you that Jessie enjoys learning things?

Ⓐ   Jessie looked closely at the quarter. It was true!

Ⓑ   Jessie studied each one. They were so interesting!

Ⓒ   After lunch, Jessie and Jon showed the quarter to Mr. Cho.

Ⓓ   That night, Jessie looked at the coins in her bank.

2. What did Jon like best about finding state quarters?

Ⓐ   finding out about horses

Ⓑ   getting his family involved in the fun

Ⓒ   winning the contest

Ⓓ   seeing how each quarter was different

3. Which word best describes Jon?

Ⓐ   sly

Ⓑ   friendly

Ⓒ   curious

Ⓓ   enthusiastic

4. How do you think Jessie will feel when she finds out Jon has more quarters?

_____

_____

5. Describe Jessie's character, using details from the passage.

_____

_____

Name _____ Date _____

Directions: Read the passage. Then use the information from the passage to answer questions 1–5.

Buried Alive

Jen and Kurt got off the chairlift and skied to the top of the trail for their last run of the day. They were both exhausted.

Suddenly, they spotted a skier slipping past a fence put up by the Ski Patrol. A sign on the fence warned DANGER–KEEP OUT!

Within minutes, a wave of snow rushed down the mountain and covered the skier. There was no sign of him as the snow continued to rumble down the slope.

"Oh, no," cried Jen, "I think that skier's in serious trouble." She reached for her radio and called the Ski Patrol.

"Ski Patrol here," her father responded.

"Dad, it's Jen. Kurt and I are standing at the top of Meadow Trail. A skier just went down the fenced-off trail. He set off an avalanche, and he's buried!"

"I'll send the rescue team," said Dad.

The team arrived within minutes. The rescue dog located the spot where the skier was buried. With small metal shovels, the rescue workers dug out the skier as quickly as they could. He seemed to be okay as they strapped him into a sled and started down the mountain.

"Great work, kids," Dad said proudly.

Name _____ Date_____

1. Where does this story take place?

(A) at a hospital   (B) in a classroom

(C) in a forest   (D) on a mountain

2. What was the problem in this story?

(A) Jen and Kurt were really tired.

(B) They could not ski the last run of the day.

(C) A skier got buried in an avalanche.

(D) The rescue team could not find the skier

3. How did Jen feel when she saw the skier disappear?

(A) excited   (B) worried

(C) angry   (D) proud

4. How did the dog help the rescue team?

_____

_____

5. What happened to the skier at the end of the story?

_____

_____

Name _____ Date _____

Directions: Read the passage. Then use the information from the passage to answer questions 1–5.

A Long Week

Mama had been sick for six days. Rebecca made Papa's supper and went to sit by Mama. "You need to eat, too," Papa said. "Come and eat supper."

Rebecca was too worried to eat, and she was so tired! She just wanted to sit and watch Mama sleep. She hoped that Mama would soon wake up and smile. But Mama had not smiled for a long time. Mama had not smiled for six whole days.

For almost a week Rebecca had cared for Mama. She washed Mama's hot face. She brought cool water for Mama to drink. She sat by Mama's bed and read her stories. But Mama did not even hear. Mama just slept and slept.

While Mama slept, Rebecca made a fire every morning. She cooked breakfast and supper for Papa. She washed the plates and cups. She fed the pigs and chickens. She watered the garden. Each time she finished a job, she told Mama. But Mama did not seem to hear.

The next morning, Mama was no better. Her fever seemed worse than ever. Papa looked worried. "We need the doctor, but it is a long ride to town. I do not want to leave you and Mama for so long."

"I will get the doctor," Rebecca said. "I can ride my pony and be back before dark."

Name _____ Date_____

1. When does this story take place?

Ⓐ a long time ago

Ⓑ a few years ago

Ⓒ in the present

Ⓓ far in the future

2. What is the main problem in this story?

Ⓐ It is a long way to town.

Ⓑ Rebecca has too much work to do.

Ⓒ Mama is very sick.

Ⓓ Papa does not want to leave Rebecca and Mama.

3. Where does this story take place?

Ⓐ in a city

Ⓑ on a farm

Ⓒ in a town

Ⓓ on a boat

4. Why was Rebecca so concerned about Mama's illness? Give two details about Mama's illness that made Rebecca worry.

_____

_____

5. What will Papa and Rebecca most likely do next?

_____

_____

Name _____ Date _____

Directions: Read the passage. Then use the information from the passage to answer questions 1–5.

The Channel Tunnel

England and France are separated by a body of water. It is called the English Channel. At one time, the only way to cross the channel was by boat. It was a long, slow trip.

In 1802, Napoleon was the ruler of France. He had an idea. He wanted to build a tunnel under the channel. It would connect France and England.

Work began nearly 100 years later. The work was hard. It was very dangerous, too. The project soon ended.

In 1957, people again talked about a tunnel. By then, people could fly from London to Paris. But plane travel was costly. Trains were cheaper. An undersea train seemed like a good idea.

The project cost too much for one country to afford. So England and France worked together. They began in 1973. But they stopped in 1975. The job was too difficult.

In 1987, work began again. Workers started in France and in England. In 1990, the two teams met. They linked the tunnel between England and France!

The first train traveled through the tunnel in 1994. Drivers once had to leave their cars behind. But now they can load them onto a train. The long boat ride has become a 30-minute train ride.

Name _____ Date_____

1. What is the main problem presented in this passage?

Ⓐ Traveling between England and France took a long time.

Ⓑ Napoleon was the ruler of France.

Ⓒ In 1957, people began talking about building a tunnel.

Ⓓ The weather in England was always cold.

2. What problems did the first tunnel builders face?

Ⓐ Only France was interested in the project.

Ⓑ Air travel was much easier.

Ⓒ The project was too hard and dangerous.

Ⓓ The idea of an undersea train was crazy.

3. Most of the details in this passage are presented in what order?

Ⓐ order of importance

Ⓑ time order

Ⓒ size order

Ⓓ alphabetical order

4. How did France and England finally get the tunnel done?

_____

_____

5. How did the tunnel solve a problem for people with cars?

_____

_____

Name _____ Date _____

Directions: Read the passage. Then use the information from the passage to answer questions 1–5.

Comics Then and Now

Do you like to read comics? Most kids do. A lot of adults read comics, too. In fact, the first comics were created for adults.

Let's go back more than 100 years. The year is 1895. You are reading a newspaper called the *New York World*. You see something new in the paper. It has words and pictures. It is called "The Yellow Kid." It is the first newspaper comic. Lots of people enjoy it. So they buy more newspapers.

Jump ahead a few years. It is about 1920. Now other papers have comics, too. One is called "Popeye." Another is called "Krazy Kat." Many people love these comics. The new comics help sell even more newspapers.

A few more years go by. Now the year is 1935. Again you see something new to read. It is the first comic book about a superhero. It is called "Superman." People begin to buy comic books. They love to read about Superman and his great powers.

Today, people still like to read comics. Most comics are funny. They make people laugh. Some comics are serious. They make people think. What kind of comics do you like?

Name _____ Date_____

1. **The writer organized the information in this passage by _____.**

Ⓐ order of importance

Ⓑ questions and answers

Ⓒ time order

Ⓓ problems and solutions

2. **Which comic came first?**

Ⓐ "Popeye"

Ⓑ "Krazy Kat"

Ⓒ "Superman"

Ⓓ "The Yellow Kid"

3. **Which sentence in the passage helps you understand that "Superman" came out after "Krazy Kat"?**

Ⓐ A few more years go by.

Ⓑ Most comics are funny.

Ⓒ It is called "Superman."

Ⓓ Now other papers have comics, too.

4. **In what part of the passage can you find out how comics changed in 1935?**

_____

_____

5. **What does the title tell you about this passage?**

_____

_____

Name _____ Date _____

Directions: Read the passage. Then use the information from the passage to answer questions 1–5.

Leonardo da Vinci: Master of Invention

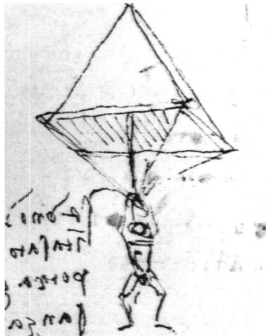

Leonardo da Vinci lived in Italy 500 years ago. You may know him as a great painter. But he was an inventor, too. He filled many notebooks with ideas and drawings for machines. These machines worked with water or air. Some of his machines were built in his lifetime. Many would not be built for hundreds of years. Many are things we use every day.

Leonardo was the first to invent a parachute. The parachute helps people float safely from a plane to Earth. Leonardo's was made of stiff linen. It was 36 feet across. Today's parachutes are made of thinner cloth. They are also much smaller. Leonardo's parachute was never made. No one knows if it worked.

Leonardo also created a fan. It was used to move air, just like fans today. But there was no electricity then. Instead, the fan could be turned by hand or by the force of water.

Another of his ideas was a flying ship. Leonardo thought this ship could carry people. It was a small ship with flapping wings. Cranks and screws made the wings move. The wings were supposed to flap like a bat's wings.

Name _____ Date_____

1. How was Leonardo da Vinci's parachute different from parachutes today?

Ⓐ It was much smaller and lighter.

Ⓑ It was bigger and made of a different cloth.

Ⓒ It was very brightly colored.

Ⓓ It had wings that flapped up and down.

2. How were all of Leonardo's machines alike?

Ⓐ They all carried people.

Ⓑ They were all made of cloth.

Ⓒ They were all modeled after animals.

Ⓓ They all worked with water or air.

3. How was Leonardo's fan different from fans used today?

Ⓐ It used electricity.

Ⓑ It did not use electricity.

Ⓒ It was much bigger than fans used today.

Ⓓ It was much smaller than fans used today.

4. How was Leonardo's fan similar to fans used today?

_____

_____

5. How is an airplane similar to Leonardo's flying ship?

_____

_____

Name _____ Date _____

Directions: Read the passage. Then use the information from the passage to answer questions 1–5.

A Different Kind of Ride

Do you like to ride your bike? Most people ride bikes in warm weather, but not many ride when it is cold outside. Almost no one rides a bicycle during the snowy winter.

One unusual man does ride on snow, and on ice, too. His name is Doug Stoup. Doug rode his bike in Antarctica! No place on Earth has more ice, snow, wind, and extreme cold.

Of course, Doug has warm clothes, and he has a special bicycle called an ice bike. Like other bikes, Doug's ice bike has two wheels, but the tires are different. They are very fat. Thin tires slip on ice. Fat tires may look funny, but they do not slip as much.

Most bikes have some plastic parts. In very cold weather, plastic can freeze and break. The ice bike has no plastic at all. Antarctica is not a good place for plastic!

In 2003, Doug tested his bike in Antarctica for a week. He rode on ice and snow, and the ice bike worked fine. It did not slip on ice or get stuck in snow. Someday, Doug hopes to ride alone across Antarctica. He wants to go all the way to the South Pole by bike.

Do you think an ice bike sounds like fun? Wait—don't give your old bike away yet! Ice bikes only work well on ice and snow, and they cost about $3,500. But they are no good at all on a warm summer day!

Name _____ Date_____

1. How are ice bikes different from most other bikes?

Ⓐ They cost more money.

Ⓑ They have more wheels.

Ⓒ They are made of plastic.

Ⓓ They are fun to slide on.

2. How are fat tires different from thin tires?

Ⓐ They are better for children's bikes.

Ⓑ They break more easily.

Ⓒ They work better in ice and snow.

Ⓓ They slip and slide a lot more.

3. Riding an ice bike is most similar to _____.

Ⓐ swimming

Ⓑ playing tennis

Ⓒ driving a race car

Ⓓ snowshoeing

4. How is Doug Stoup different from most other people who ride bikes?

_____

_____

5. How is Doug Stoup's bike different from most other bikes?

_____

_____

Name _____ Date _____

Directions: Read the passage. Then use the information from the passage to answer questions 1–5.

The Most Exciting Job in the World

Are you curious? Do you like to learn new things? Then you would love my job. I am a space scientist. At work, I ask questions and look for answers. Every day I learn something new. Being a scientist is the most exciting job in the world! It's an important job, too. I can't wait to get to work every day.

My group is studying the planet Saturn. There is so much we need to find out! We want to learn about Saturn's rings. We want to learn about Saturn's dozens of moons. Right now we are studying Titan. Titan is Saturn's biggest moon. Not long ago, we sent a probe that landed on Titan. The probe was about as big as a car. It did a wonderful job. It sent us a lot of information. It also sent pictures.

We thought the probe would work for only a few minutes. But it worked for hours! That was very exciting. Now scientists are studying the information. It will take many years to study it all.

Does that sound like a long time? To a scientist, it is not long at all. We waited a long time to get the information. It took seven years for the probe to reach Titan. A good scientist must be curious. A good scientist must be patient, too!

1. Which sentence from the passage states a fact?

Ⓐ   Then you would love my job.

Ⓑ   I am a space scientist.

Ⓒ   Being a scientist is the most exciting job in the world!

Ⓓ   It's an important job, too.

2. Which sentence from the passage states an opinion?

Ⓐ   It took seven years for the probe to reach Titan.

Ⓑ   It did a wonderful job.

Ⓒ   Now scientists are studying the information.

Ⓓ   My group is studying the planet Saturn.

3. Which sentence is an opinion?

Ⓐ   The space probe is about the size of a car.

Ⓑ   The planet Saturn has dozens of moons.

Ⓒ   Saturn is the most interesting planet.

Ⓓ   Titan is Saturn's biggest moon.

4. Give one fact and one opinion from the third paragraph.

_____

_____

_____

5. According to the writer of this passage, what makes a good scientist?

_____

_____

_____

Name _____ Date _____

Directions: *Read the passage. Then use the information from the passage to answer questions 1–5.*

New Video Fun from Giant Games

Get ready for some fun! Buy **Build-A-World** from Giant Games. This is the new video game everyone wants to play. Dads, moms, and kids all love **Build-A-World**. Here are some things players can do with this fun game.

- Make a special place. You can build a town. You can make houses, parks, lakes, and more.

- Create and name characters. You can make a big family or a small one. You can make neighbors, friends, and even pets.

- Make some vehicles. You'll want to travel in your new world. You can make bikes, cars, and trains. You can even make a rocket!

- Play alone or play with others. **Build-A-World** is lots of fun to play alone. It's even more fun to play with others.

Are you a sports nut? You will want **Build-A-Team**. **Build-A-Team** is a ton of fun! Here is what you can do with this game.

- Make a sports team. Pick your sport and give your team a name.

- Pick your players and name them, too.

- Make team uniforms.

- Play to win!

Build-A-World and **Build-A-Team** cost $30.00 each. Or you can buy both great games for only $50.00. Try them both! You'll be glad you did. The whole family will love them!

Giant Games makes games in Chicago, Illinois.

You can buy Giant Games in stores or online.

We send games all over the world.

Name _____ Date_____

1. Which sentence states an opinion?

Ⓐ You can make a sports team with **Build-A-Team**.

Ⓑ It costs $50.00 to buy both video games.

Ⓒ Players can make houses and cars using **Build-A-World**.

Ⓓ **Build-A-World** is lots of fun to play alone.

2. Which sentence from the passage states a fact?

Ⓐ Dads, moms, and kids all love **Build-A-World**.

Ⓑ **Build-A-World** and **Build-A-Team** cost $30.00 each.

Ⓒ It's even more fun to play with others.

Ⓓ The whole family will love them!

3. Which sentence from the passage states a fact?

Ⓐ You'll be glad you did.

Ⓑ **Build-A-Team** is a ton of fun!

Ⓒ You'll want to travel in your new world.

Ⓓ Giant Games makes games in Chicago, Illinois.

4. Write one sentence from the passage that is a fact and tell why it is a fact.

_____

_____

5. Write one sentence from the passage that states an opinion and tell why it is an opinion.

_____

_____

Name _____ Date _____

Directions: Read the passage. Then use the information from the passage to answer questions 1–5.

Big Bad Wolf's Bad Hair Day

SETTING: Granny's house and Myra's Hair Salon next door

CHARACTERS: Big Bad Wolf, Myra, and Little Red Riding Hood

(A small cottage stands on the left side of the stage. Myra's salon is on the right. BIG BAD WOLF, in a dress and bonnet, runs from the cottage into the salon.)

BIG BAD WOLF: Quick! I need a shampoo and a haircut!

MYRA: Sure, but what's the hurry?

BIG BAD WOLF: *(sliding into the chair)* I'm expecting Little Red Riding Hood any minute now. I have to hurry back to eat—er, I mean greet her.

MYRA: *(surprised)* Is that you, Granny? I didn't recognize you. You sound exactly like a wolf! *(She looks as if she's just figured something out.)* Let's get you under the dryer now! *(BIG BAD WOLF moves to the hair dryer. He starts reading a magazine. LITTLE RED RIDING HOOD enters, but BIG BAD WOLF doesn't notice her.)* Little Red Riding Hood, that's the Big Bad Wolf over there. He's wearing your granny's clothes and pretending to be her.

LITTLE RED RIDING HOOD: I'd better check on Granny! *(She runs into the cottage. Then she runs back to the salon.)* Granny's okay, Myra.

MYRA: *(turning off the hair dryer)* You couldn't fool me, you nasty wolf.

BIG BAD WOLF: *(howling loudly as he leaves)* Myra, I won't be leaving you a tip!

Name _____ Date_____

1. What does Big Bad Wolf do in the story that a real wolf might do?

Ⓐ He wears a dress.

Ⓑ He gets a shampoo.

Ⓒ He howls loudly.

Ⓓ He reads a magazine.

2. Which of these things could NOT really happen?

Ⓐ A girl visits her grandmother.

Ⓑ A wolf reads a magazine.

Ⓒ A girl talks to a hairdresser.

Ⓓ A wolf gets hungry.

3. Which of these is make-believe?

Ⓐ A wolf talks.

Ⓑ A wolf runs.

Ⓒ A girl runs into a cottage.

Ⓓ A woman uses a hair dryer.

4. Name one thing that happens in this play that could happen in real life.

_____

_____

5. How can you tell that this story is make-believe?

_____

_____

Name _____ Date _____

Directions: *Read the passage. Then use the information from the passage to answer questions 1–5.*

Grandfather Bear's Promise

Did you know that once, long ago, bears had long tails? Bears were proud of their beautiful, fluffy tails. Then one day, Grandfather Bear woke up early. It was still winter, and he should have been sleeping his long sleep.

Who knows why he woke early? Mr. Fox was passing by, and maybe he was too noisy. Mr. Fox was singing and skipping. He carried a big fish he had stolen from a shop. Grandfather Bear smelled that fish, and it sure smelled good.

"My friend, are you hungry?" Mr. Fox asked. "Go down to the lake. Break the ice and put your tail in the hole. When you pull up your tail, you will see your supper!"

Grandfather Bear was sleepy, but now he was hungry. He ran to the lake, broke the ice, and put in his tail. The cold water hurt, but Grandfather Bear did not give up. "If Mr. Fox can do this, I can, too," he said.

A long time passed, but no fish came. Grandfather Bear waited so long that he fell asleep. When he awoke, his tail was stuck in the ice. "Ouch! A big fish is holding my tail!" he cried. "Please let go! If you let go, I promise not to eat you up!"

The poor old bear pulled his tail as hard as he could. At last he pulled free and ran home. But the beautiful tail stayed behind, stuck in the ice.

Grandfather Bear kept his promise. Never again did he eat fish for supper. Never again did any bear have a long, beautiful tail.

Name _____ Date_____

1. What does the bear do in this story that a real bear might do?

Ⓐ He looks for his supper.   Ⓑ He talks with a fox.

Ⓒ He loses his tail in the ice.   Ⓓ He makes a promise.

2. Which of these is make-believe?

Ⓐ A bear is sleepy.   Ⓑ A fish smells good.

Ⓒ A fox sings and skips.   Ⓓ A bear wakes up.

3. Which of these could really happen?

Ⓐ A fox teaches a bear how to fish.

Ⓑ A fish holds a bear's tail.

Ⓒ A bear sleeps for a long time.

Ⓓ A fox steals from a shop.

4. How can you tell this story is not real?

_____

_____

5. Give two reasons why the events in the last paragraph could not really happen.

_____

_____

_____

_____

Name _____ Date _____

Directions: Read the passage. Then use the information from the passage to answer questions 1–5.

Growing Up Shawnee

Long ago, the Shawnee lived in the eastern part of what is now the United States. These Native Americans lived together in bands. They hunted, farmed, and gathered wild food. From a young age, Shawnee children learned the skills they needed for this way of life.

A Shawnee baby spent only a few weeks at home with its mother. Then the mother returned to her work. She strapped the baby into a wooden cradle. She wore the cradle on her back as she gathered food or farmed. In about six months, the cradle was set aside. Then the baby could crawl about with other young children while its mother worked. As Shawnee children grew a little older, they learned to help the women with their work.

By the age of nine, Shawnee boys and girls spent most of their time apart. While their fathers hunted deer and bears, boys took hunting lessons from older men. Girls stayed with their mothers and learned different skills. Sewing and cooking lessons took up much of their time. Girls were taught to plant and harvest corn, beans, and other crops. They also learned to tan animal hides and make pots out of clay.

Name _____ Date_____

1. What can you tell about the Shawnee from this passage?

Ⓐ   The Shawnee lived on the plains.

Ⓑ   Mothers and girls worked hard.

Ⓒ   The Shawnee ate only meat and corn.

Ⓓ   Fathers made clothes from animal hides.

2. Who taught Shawnee girls the skills they needed to know?

Ⓐ   their older sisters

Ⓑ   their fathers

Ⓒ   their older brothers

Ⓓ   their mothers

3. In Shawnee villages, who did most of the hunting?

Ⓐ   mothers

Ⓑ   older men

Ⓒ   fathers

Ⓓ   young boys

4. After the age of nine, why did Shawnee boys and girls spend most of their time apart?

_____

_____

5. Write a sentence from the passage that shows that Shawnee girls worked hard.

_____

_____

Name ————————————————————— Date ——————————

Directions: Read the passage. Then use the information from the passage to answer questions 1–5.

Trains of the Future?

Have you ever played with magnets? If so, you know that a magnet attracts metal. What happens if you put the same ends of two different magnets together? The poles push away from each other.

An electromagnet works like a magnet does, but it uses electricity. Picture a battery. It has positive and negative ends. Electrons collect on the negative end. When you hook both ends to a wire, electrons rush toward the positive side. This causes a small magnetic field. When you unhook the wire, the electrons stop moving through it.

The newest kind of train works with electromagnets. The train has big magnets under it. The train runs on a track that has electric coils along it. This train is a maglev train.

As the train runs on the track, magnets push and pull it along. This force also lifts the train. The train rises up, or levitates, an inch or two above the track. It doesn't touch the track at all. This lets it run at super speeds.

Germany, Japan, and China have made maglev trains. The trains run at more than half the speed of a plane. A maglev train could run from one coast of the United States to the other in about ten hours.

Right now, maglev trains are expensive. Some people think they are not practical. But that may change. The cost may come down. If so, maglev trains may become the trains of the future.

1. What happens when the wire that connects both ends of a battery is unhooked?

Ⓐ The magnetic field disappears.

Ⓑ The battery attracts metal.

Ⓒ The magnetic field increases.

Ⓓ The electrons fall out of the battery.

2. Based on the passage, what is true of trains that run on tracks?

Ⓐ They cross the United States in ten hours.

Ⓑ They are not used any longer in China or Japan.

Ⓒ They cannot run as fast as maglev trains.

Ⓓ They cost nearly as much as maglev trains.

3. From this passage, what can you conclude about Germany, Japan, and China?

Ⓐ They use trains more than cars and trucks.

Ⓑ They do not have room for more trains.

Ⓒ They have spent a lot of money on maglev trains.

Ⓓ They will not sell their trains.

4. Which clues from the passage tell you that most countries will not have maglev trains for a long time?

_____

_____

5. How can a maglev train run above the track and not on the track? Use details from the passage to explain.

_____

_____

Name_____ Date _____

Directions: Read the passage. Then use the information from the passage to answer questions 1–5.

A Sweet Time of Year

In parts of New England, the snow in the woods begins to melt in March. When the sun gets warm enough, something special happens. The sap in the maple trees starts to run! It flows from the roots up through the trees. This is the time to make maple syrup. If you eat pancakes with real maple syrup, you know how sweet that syrup tastes!

In New England, many people make maple syrup. There are several steps in making it. First, you have to tap the tree. This means that you drill a hole in the trunk of a sugar maple tree. Then you put in a tap or a tube. The sap flows from the tree into a bucket. When the bucket is full, workers pour the sap into a big vat. The vat is used to boil the sap over a fire.

As it boils, the sap gets thicker. Before long, most of the water has boiled off. What is left is good, thick syrup. It smells wonderful, and it tastes great. Some makers like to pour hot maple syrup on homemade doughnuts and eat them as they work. Others make maple sugar candy.

To make one gallon of syrup takes 40 to 60 gallons of sap. Making syrup is hard work. But syrup makers love this time of year. The season only lasts about three weeks, and making syrup is fun. When the trees begin to bud, the season ends.

In the United States, Vermont makes more maple syrup than any other state. It produces about 400,000 gallons of syrup every year. New York makes about 200,000 gallons. Several other states make syrup, too.

1. This passage was written mainly to _____.

Ⓐ   tell how maple syrup is made

Ⓑ   give information about Vermont

Ⓒ   tell how to cook pancakes

Ⓓ   make people plant more trees

2. The author probably mentioned pancakes in this passage because he wanted to suggest that _____.

Ⓐ   pancakes are good for you Ⓑ   many people like maple syrup

Ⓒ   pancakes are easy to make Ⓓ   eating breakfast is important

3. The author probably mentioned Vermont and New York in this passage to _____.

Ⓐ   make people want to visit those states

Ⓑ   tell how much maple syrup costs

Ⓒ   describe how people eat maple syrup

Ⓓ   tell where maple syrup is made

4. What does the author think of maple syrup season? Give a detail from the passage to support your answer.

_____

_____

5. What is the author's opinion of maple syrup? Give a detail from the passage to support your answer.

_____

_____

Name _____ Date _____

Directions: *Read the passage. Then use the information from the passage to answer questions 1–5.*

From the Police Chief's Mailbag

Dear Chief Norman,

I have lived in town all of my life. I went to Elmwood Elementary School for six years. At first I walked to school with my brother. When we were older, we rode our bikes to school. We both loved that!

Now I am a parent, and my children go to Elmwood School. They often beg me to let them ride bikes to school. Chief Norman, I want them to ride. I wish they could! But today there are so many cars in town. There is much more traffic than in the past. To get to school, Tim and Tonya must cross Great Plain Road. They cannot cross this busy street alone. No child can. A police officer could help children cross safely. I have talked with many parents in my neighborhood. We need your help. Our children need your help.

You can help in one of these ways. Hire a crossing guard to help children cross. Or send a police officer to help the children. I know the police work hard to keep people safe. This is a way to keep our children safe.

My number is 555-1530. I will wait for your call. Thank you for reading my letter.

Yours truly,

Lily Cho

Name _____ Date_____

1. Lily Cho wrote this letter because she wanted to _____.

Ⓐ get a job as a crossing guard

Ⓑ thank the police chief for his work

Ⓒ get someone to help children cross a busy street

Ⓓ tell people she had lived in town all her life

2. Why does Mrs. Cho think that police should help children cross the street?

Ⓐ It is part of their job of keeping people safe.

Ⓑ No one else can do it.

Ⓒ She loved to ride her bike to school when she was a child.

Ⓓ The parents are all too busy.

3. Lily Cho hopes that Chief Norman will _____.

Ⓐ lower the speed limit for drivers

Ⓑ make it safe for children to ride to school

Ⓒ cut down on the traffic in town

Ⓓ teach children how to cross streets safely

4. Why did Mrs. Cho include her telephone number in the letter?

_____

_____

5. How does Mrs. Cho feel about children riding bikes to school?

_____

_____

Name _____ Date _____

Directions: Read the passage. Then use the information from the passage to answer questions 1–5.

The Tundra

The Arctic tundra is near the North Pole. It is the coldest biome, or habitat, in the world. The layer of soil below the surface is always frozen. There are no trees. The temperature ranges from 20°F to minus 70°F. The growing season lasts only 50 to 60 days. This is why the biome has little plant life. Grass, moss, and sedge grow here.

Several kinds of animals live in the tundra. Some, like reindeer and rabbits, eat plants. Others, like polar bears and wolves, eat meat. They hunt the plant-eating animals. The Arctic tundra is home to some insects and birds as well.

The Arctic tundra is changing. People are causing the changes. They drive snowmobiles and cars into the area. They run over the plants. It takes many years for the plants to grow back. Meanwhile, many animals lack food. Their numbers are getting smaller.

People are also hunting in the tundra. They are killing seals, polar bears, and reindeer. But laws are being passed to limit the hunting of animals.

As you can see, tundra wildlife is fragile. People must take care of this habitat. If they don't, many species of plants and animals could become extinct.

Name _____ Date_____

1. What causes the tundra to have little plant life?

Ⓐ There are no trees. Ⓑ The growing season is short.

Ⓒ Rabbits and bears live there. Ⓓ People drive snowmobiles.

2. What is the effect of plant life being destroyed?

Ⓐ Animals do not have enough food to eat.

Ⓑ People drive snowmobiles into this ecosystem.

Ⓒ Moss grows in the tundra.

Ⓓ The temperature drops to between 20°F and minus 70°F.

3. What will happen if people do not take care of the tundra habitat?

Ⓐ Polar bears and wolves will hunt the plant-eating animals.

Ⓑ The growing season will last only 50 to 60 days.

Ⓒ Cars and snowmobiles will break down in the tundra.

Ⓓ Many plants and animals will become extinct.

4. Why is the Arctic tundra changing? Give two reasons found in the passage.

_____

_____

5. What effect does driving snowmobiles have on the tundra?

_____

_____

Name _____ Date _____

Directions: Read the passage. Then use the information from the passage to answer questions 1–5.

Helping Some Big Babies

Is there a baby in your family? Then you know babies need lots of care. They cannot take care of themselves when they are little.

Elephant babies are not little. Still, they need lots of care. They cannot take care of themselves. That's why Daphne Sheldrick started an orphanage in Africa. It is an orphanage for elephants! Daphne lives in Kenya near Tsavo National Park. She runs the orphanage at her home.

Zoe is a young elephant. When Zoe came to the orphanage, she was just two weeks old. Zoe was hungry. She needed good food and good care. Zoe lived at the orphanage for a year. She got bigger and stronger. Then workers took her to the park. There they help Zoe learn to find her own food. They keep her in a safe, fenced-in place at night. Someday Zoe will go and live in the wild. Workers will know when she is ready to go.

Why are there orphans like Zoe? Sometimes adult elephants go onto farms and harm plants. Farmers kill some of the elephants. Hunters kill even more. They sell the elephants' ivory. People make things from ivory.

Daphne wants people to stop using ivory. Then no one would buy it from the hunters. Maybe there would be no more need for the elephant orphanage.

Name _____ Date_____

1. Why did Daphne Sheldrick start an orphanage for elephants?

(A) She lives near a park.

(B) Elephant babies cannot take care of themselves.

(C) She likes all kinds of animals.

(D) Zoe was just two weeks old, and she was hungry.

2. Farmers in Africa sometimes kill elephants because _____.

(A) they like to hunt

(B) they want to make things from ivory

(C) the elephants hurt plants

(D) the elephants need lots of care

3. For Zoe, what was the effect of living at the orphanage?

(A) She went to live in the wild.

(B) She got bigger and stronger.

(C) A hunter wanted her ivory.

(D) She was lost and hungry.

4. Why are there orphan elephants in Africa? Give two reasons found in the passage.

_____

_____

5. If no one used ivory anymore, what would probably happen to elephants?

_____

_____

Name _____ Date _____

Directions: *Read the passage. Then use the information from the passage to answer questions 1–5.*

The Great Pyramid

The Great Pyramid was built by King Khufu in Egypt. Only a few things are known about him. He lived around 2500 B.C. He ruled for about 20 years. Some people believe that he was a bad ruler. They think he made his people build the pyramid. No one knows if this is true.

The Great Pyramid rises 449 feet above the plain at Giza. It is the largest pyramid. The base of the pyramid is huge. It covers seven city blocks. Each side of the base is 754 feet long.

Early visitors stole nearly everything from the Great Pyramid. When scientists found it in the 1800s, the beautiful decorations were gone. One thing was found nearby. It was a large, wooden boat called the Sun Boat. The Egyptians thought the boat would carry Khufu into the next life.

The Great Pyramid is not as great as it once was. When it was built, it was 30 feet higher than it is now. Time and weather have worn it down. Still, it is an amazing thing to see.

Name _____ Date_____

1. What is the stated main idea in this passage?

Ⓐ   The Great Pyramid was built by King Khufu of Egypt.

Ⓑ   Early visitors stole nearly everything from the Great Pyramid.

Ⓒ   King Khufu made his people build a pyramid.

Ⓓ   Blocks of stone were used to build the pyramid.

2. Which detail supports the main idea in paragraph two that the Great Pyramid is very tall?

Ⓐ   Its base is as large as seven city blocks.

Ⓑ   It is the largest pyramid.

Ⓒ   It rises 449 feet above the plain at Giza.

Ⓓ   It covers seven city blocks.

3. What is the stated main idea in the last paragraph?

Ⓐ   Time and weather have worn down the Great Pyramid.

Ⓑ   The Great Pyramid is not as great as it once was.

Ⓒ   The Great Pyramid is an amazing thing to see.

Ⓓ   The Great Pyramid was once 30 feet higher.

4. What is the stated main idea in paragraph three?

_____

_____

5. What details support the idea that few things are known about King Khufu?

_____

_____

Name_____ Date _____

Directions: Read the passage. Then use the information from the passage to answer questions 1–5.

Become a Cloud Watcher

Look up at the sky. Most likely, you will see clouds. All clouds are made of water, snow, or ice. But not all clouds are the same. If you learn about clouds, you can tell a lot about the weather. Here are some kinds of clouds you are likely to see.

On fair, sunny days you may see cumulus clouds. These clouds are fat and puffy. They look like soft cotton floating in the sky. When you see cumulus clouds, the weather will stay fair.

Cumulonimbus clouds are bigger and much taller. If you see these dark clouds, watch out. They bring bad weather. They will surely bring rain or hail. They often bring thunder and lightning. Sometimes they bring dangerous storms called tornadoes.

Some clouds are quite low in the sky. They are called stratus clouds. These low clouds may even hide the tops of tall buildings. When you see stratus clouds, expect some light rain. In the winter, stratus clouds may bring snow.

Cirrus clouds are thin and wispy. These pretty clouds are very high in the sky. They are made of tiny bits of ice. It is fun to watch them move, curl and change shape. Look for cirrus clouds when the weather is fair.

Become a cloud watcher. Notice each cloud's shape and size. Then you will know what kind of cloud it is. You will know what kind of weather to expect. Best of all, you will not miss the beauty of the clouds in the sky.

Name _____ Date_____

1. What is this passage mostly about?
(A) different kinds of clouds   (B) learning about science
(C) sunny days and rainy days   (D) how clouds are made

2. What is the main idea in paragraph one?
(A) More people should look at the sky every day and
    see the clouds.
(B) If you look up, you will always see clouds.
(C) There are different kinds of clouds, and they tell about
    the weather.
(D) Clouds are made of water, snow, or ice.

3. Which sentence best states the main idea of this passage?
(A) Certain kinds of clouds are sure to bring rain.
(B) You should know what kind of weather to expect.
(C) Some clouds are better and prettier than others.
(D) It is enjoyable and worthwhile to be a cloud watcher.

**4. Give three details from the passage to support the idea that
you should watch out when you see cumulonimbus clouds.**

_____

_____

_____

_____

5. What would be another good title for this passage?

_____

_____

Name _____ Date _____

Directions: Read the passage. Then use the information from the passage to answer questions 1–5.

Making a Budget

A budget is a plan for getting, spending, and saving money. Follow these steps to make a budget.

First, get a notebook. Each page will be for a different week. Write the date at the top of the page. Then draw and label a chart as shown below.

In the first box, write down all the money you expect to get: exactly how much it will be and where it will come from. In the second box, write down where this money will go. Start with all necessary expenses. Then write down things you would like to spend money on. Last, write down how much money you plan to save, if any.

This is your plan, which may or may not work out. Keep track of what really happens in the boxes on the right.

Budgets are a great way to track your money. If you get into the habit of keeping a budget now, you will learn to manage your money for the future.

What I Planned	**What Really Happened**
MONEY IN—PLANNED	MONEY IN—REAL
Allowance $5	Allowance $5
Money for yard work $3	Money for yard work . . . . . $0 (rained)
Birthday money $15	Birthday money $10
Total $23	**Total** $15
MONEY OUT—PLANNED	MONEY OUT—REAL
Present for Grandma $10	Present for Grandma $12
Snack at pool $3	Savings $3
Savings $10	
Total $23	**Total** $15

Name _____ Date_____

1. What should you do first to make a budget?

Ⓐ Draw a chart.   Ⓑ Write the date.

Ⓒ Get a notebook.   Ⓓ Label the chart.

2. After you make a chart for your budget, what should you do next?

Ⓐ Write the date on each page.

Ⓑ Make a list of things you want to buy.

Ⓒ Estimate how much money you can save each week.

Ⓓ Write the amount of money you expect to get.

3. What will happen if you take in more money than you spend?

Ⓐ You will need a new notebook.

Ⓑ You will have money left over.

Ⓒ You will become rich.

Ⓓ You will make some new friends.

4. When you make your budget, what is the first thing you should write in the box for MONEY OUT — PLANNED?

_____

_____

5. With this kind of budget, what should you do at the end of each week?

_____

_____

Name _____ Date _____

Directions: Read the passage. Then use the information from the passage to answer questions 1–5.

All Mixed Up

Water is a clear, colorless, action-packed liquid. Perform this experiment to see for yourself.

What You Need:
small jar filled with water
red and yellow food coloring

What You Do:

1. Set the jar in a place where you can leave it for several hours.

2. Add two drops of red food coloring and two drops of yellow food coloring to the water. Notice how the food coloring sinks to the bottom of the jar.

3. Check the jar in three or four hours to see how the water has changed.

What Happens:
You will find a jar of orange water!

Why It Happens:
Food coloring is heavier than water, so it sinks to the bottom of the jar when first added. Water is made up of tiny particles that are always moving. As these particles bounce around in the jar, they cause the food-coloring particles to mix together.

After you have done the experiment, be sure to clean up properly.

1. Which step comes first?

Ⓐ   Put red food coloring in the jar.

Ⓑ   Check the jar in three hours.

Ⓒ   Set the jar in its chosen place.

Ⓓ   Put yellow food coloring in the jar.

2. Just after you add the red food coloring, what happens to it?

Ⓐ   It turns orange.

Ⓑ   It mixes with the yellow food coloring.

Ⓒ   It starts to move upward.

Ⓓ   It sinks to the bottom of the jar.

3. What should you do three or four hours after you start the experiment?

Ⓐ   Check to see how the water has changed.

Ⓑ   Move the jar to a different place.

Ⓒ   Stir the food coloring and water together.

Ⓓ   Add some drops of orange food coloring.

4. What happens in the jar after the food coloring sinks?

_____

_____

5. What should you do after the water in the jar turns orange?

_____

_____

Name _____ Date _____

Directions: Read the passage. Then use the information from the passage to answer questions 1–5.

Just Not Herself

The phone call came the day after Hank put up the posters. "Your cat's in my yard," a woman's voice said. "Please come get her right now!"

"Is she a gray-and-brown tiger with white paws?" Hank asked anxiously.

"Just like the cat in the poster!" the woman snapped. "Come get her!"

Hank ran two blocks to the woman's house. He picked up the crouching Snowshoes and said, "She must be starving after being lost for three days."

But at home, Snowshoes ignored her cat food. That night, instead of sleeping on Hank's bed, Snowshoes howled at the door. Finally, Hank let her out. "Snowshoes is just not herself," he decided.

The next day, Dr. Ward examined Snowshoes and told Hank not to worry. But Hank was not convinced.

When Hank got home, his mother met him at the door. "We're going to bring that cat to the animal shelter," she said. "They'll find a home for her."

"Mom!" cried Hank. "Dr. Ward said she'll be herself in a few days. Please don't make me give her up!"

Mom laughed and said, "The real Snowshoes came home while you were gone. She's on her third can of cat food and is purring away!"

Name _____ Date_____

1. How did the woman feel about the cat in her yard?

Ⓐ She thought the cat was beautiful.

Ⓑ She disliked the cat.

Ⓒ She wanted to keep the cat.

Ⓓ She felt sorry for the cat.

2. When Hank brought Snowshoes home, the cat seemed _____.

Ⓐ frisky   Ⓑ hungry

Ⓒ tired   Ⓓ unfriendly

3. Dr. Ward is the kind of doctor who _____.

Ⓐ takes care of animals

Ⓑ visits people in their homes

Ⓒ sets people's broken bones

Ⓓ works only with young children

4. Name two kinds of information that were given in Hank's poster.

_____

_____

5. Why do you think Hank named his cat Snowshoes?

_____

_____

Name _____ Date _____

Directions: Read the passage. Then use the information from the passage to answer questions 1–5.

Harriet the Tortoise

Every November 15, the Australia Zoo had a birthday party for a tortoise named Harriet. She was the oldest known living creature on Earth.

Harriet was born about 1830. She lived in the Galápagos Islands. When she was about five years old, Harriet was taken to England. Twelve years later, she was moved to a zoo in Australia. For more than 100 years, visitors rode on Harriet's back. Some even carved their name into her shell.

In 1988, Harriet moved to a new home. There, visitors were not allowed to touch her. They could not ride on her back. Only zookeepers and workers could touch her.

Harriet lived in comfort. She was fed a healthful diet of plants. The enclosure she lived in had grass, shady trees, and a small pool. It also had a special cave where she could stay cool on warm days.

Other animals at the zoo were more exciting than Harriet. But when visitors found out her age, they fell in love with her. And every November 15, they sang "Happy Birthday" to her. Harriet died in 2006. She was 176 years old.

Name _____ Date_____

1. **What can you infer from this passage about Harriet in her home in Australia?**
   (A) The people at the zoo cared about Harriet.
   (B) Visitors to the zoo enjoyed feeding Harriet.
   (C) Harriet liked to eat bugs and small animals.
   (D) Harriet lived on an island in the ocean.

2. **Which clue from the passage supports the inference that people are impressed by something that is old?**
   (A) Every November, the Australia Zoo had a birthday party.
   (B) Harriet was born about 1830.
   (C) Other animals at the zoo were more exciting than Harriet.
   (D) When visitors found out her age, they fell in love with her.

3. **Which inference can be made about Harriet's life at the Australia Zoo?**
   (A) She enjoyed the birthday parties the zoo gave her.
   (B) She was more protected than she was in the past.
   (C) She did not mind giving rides to zoo visitors.
   (D) She had to find her own food there.

4. **Which clues from the passage support the inference that Harriet lived a healthy life?**

   _____

   _____

5. **What is the most likely reason that visitors were not allowed to ride on Harriet anymore?**

   _____

   _____

Name _____ Date _____

Directions: *Read the passage. Then use the information from the passage to answer questions 1–5.*

She Says, He Says

Dear Diary,

Help! Mom and Mrs. Newman made plans to spend tomorrow at the beach. That means I have to spend the day with Bennie Newman, and that means he's going to realize that I can't swim!

I know what will happen. When I put on my life jacket, Bennie's going to smirk and say, "Looks like Brainy Janey flunked swimming class!" Then he's going to spread the word to all his cool friends, and they'll tease me, too.

Mom says I'm being silly. "Lots of kids your age are still learning how to swim," she told me. "If Bennie has a problem with that, just ignore him."

Okay, Mom, I can tell it's been a long time since you've embarrassed yourself in front of the coolest kid in school.

Dear Diary,

I can see it now. Janey Ames is going to swim out to the raft and then wave and yell, "The water's great, Bennie! Why don't you come in?"

So I'll wade in and do my ridiculous doggie paddle, and she'll laugh her head off. In a few days, all her brainy friends will know that I can't swim.

So I guess I'll just try to fool her. I'll bring all my sand toys to the beach and start building a sand castle, and I'll casually tell Janey I'd rather build than swim. Of course, she'll probably start building her own castle, and she'll make it bigger and better than mine.

It's going to be a completely awful day!

1. From reading the first part of the passage, what can you predict about the next day?

Ⓐ Bennie and Janey will take swimming lessons together.

Ⓑ Janey will forget her life jacket.

Ⓒ Bennie and Janey will meet at the beach.

Ⓓ Janey will save Bennie from drowning.

2. How will Janey feel when she first sees Bennie at the beach?

Ⓐ embarrassed   Ⓑ afraid

Ⓒ confident   Ⓓ sad

3. How will Bennie probably feel when he learns Janey's secret?

Ⓐ sorry   Ⓑ upset

Ⓒ amused   Ⓓ relieved

4. What will Bennie most likely bring with him?

_____

5. What will Bennie and Janey find out about each other?

_____

_____

Name_____ Date_____

Directions: Read the passage. Then use the information from the passage to answer questions 1–5.

Giving Robots a Sense of Touch

Many robots can move and "see" with light sensors. Today, scientists want to help robots "feel."

Scientists have made a robot finger out of a special kind of plastic. This plastic can sense changes in pressure or electrical current. The robot finger can sense the weight of an object. It can change its grip to fit the object, too. If the object is heavy, the finger holds it tightly. If it is light, the finger holds it gently.

Engineers are working on robots with a sense of touch. One is building a robot finger with a ball at the tip. The ball will roll over an object. It will tell the difference between smooth and rough surfaces.

Some of these fingers are hooked up to gloves worn by humans. These robots send information they feel to the gloves. Then the humans wearing the gloves can feel what the robots feel. This could help in exploring space.

Another team has made a robot that looks like a sea creature. It is called Public Anemone. This creature can already move and see. Now the scientists are making its "skin." The skin will be able to sense heat, pressure, and movement.

Robot research is not just for fun. Robots can do jobs that are too hard, dangerous, or dull for humans. To do these jobs, robots must move, see, and feel.

Name _____ Date _____

1. What will likely happen if a robot finger lifts a feather?

Ⓐ It will drop the feather.   Ⓑ It will use a gentle grip.

Ⓒ It will hold it tightly.   Ⓓ It will break the feather.

2. Based on the passage, which task is a job robots might do in the future?

Ⓐ train dogs   Ⓑ design houses

Ⓒ place explosives   Ⓓ paint portraits

3. If a future robot touched a rock on Mars, what might happen?

Ⓐ The rock would send electricity through the robot.

Ⓑ Plastic would cause the robot to explode.

Ⓒ It would break the rock with its fingertips.

Ⓓ A scientist on Earth wearing a glove would feel the rock's texture.

4. According to the passage, what will Public Anemone soon be able to do?

_____

_____

5. In the future, what kinds of "dull" jobs will robots do? Describe at least two such jobs.

_____

_____

Name_____ Date _____

Directions: Read the passage. Then use the information from the passage to answer questions 1–5.

A Look at Lakes

A lake is a body of water surrounded by land. When a hollow fills with water, a lake is made. Some lakes form in old volcanoes. One such lake is Crater Lake in Oregon. Many lakes form in holes left by glaciers. People also make lakes by building dams. Lake Mead is one lake made this way. It was formed when Hoover Dam was built on the Colorado River.

Lakes fill up with water from rivers and streams that run into them. Rain and melted snow also help fill up lakes. The water that runs into lakes often flows above ground. It is easy to see. But some lakes seem to fill up as if by magic. These lakes are fed by springs and streams that flow underground.

Most lakes have freshwater, but some are salty, like the ocean. Great Salt Lake in Utah is salty. Saltwater lakes are found in hot, dry places. Heat causes the water in these lakes to evaporate. Small amounts of salt in the water are left behind. Over many years, the salt builds up in the lake.

Lakes don't last forever. A lake may dry up if the climate gets hotter. When this happens, more water evaporates than flows in. Other lakes dry up because the rivers and streams that feed them change course. Some disappear because they slowly fill up with mud and plants.

Name _____ Date_____

1. Which sentence best summarizes what this passage is about?

Ⓐ It describes one lake.

Ⓑ It compares two lakes.

Ⓒ It explains why lakes are important.

Ⓓ It tells how lakes form and change.

2. Which detail should be included in a summary of the first paragraph?

Ⓐ Lakes may form in holes left by volcanoes or glaciers.

Ⓑ Lakes fed by underground streams are quite cold.

Ⓒ Many lakes are kept filled by streams running into them.

Ⓓ Hoover Dam was built across the Colorado River.

3. Read these two sentences from the passage.

But some lakes seem to fill up as if by magic. These lakes are fed by springs and streams that flow underground.

Which is the best paraphrase of these sentences?

Ⓐ Some lakes are magical lakes underground.

Ⓑ These lakes fill by magic from springs and streams.

Ⓒ Some lakes are fed by underground springs or streams.

Ⓓ Springs and streams sometimes form lakes underground.

4. Write one or two sentences that summarize the third paragraph.

_____

_____

5. Rewrite these sentences in your own words.

A lake may dry up if the climate gets hotter. When this happens, more water evaporates than flows in.

_____

_____

Name —————————————————————— Date ——————————

Directions: Read the passage. Then use the information from the passage to answer questions 1–5.

Measuring Time

People are very interested in time. They have been measuring time for thousands of years. The first "clocks" were sticks in the ground. The sticks cast shadows when the sun was out. The shadows helped people know what time it was. Then, around 1500 B.C. in Egypt, the sundial was invented. It also used the sun to tell time. It was more precise than the stick clock. People used sundials for 3,000 years.

The water clock was used around the same time. It was a stone pot with sloping sides. Water dripped out of a hole in the bottom. The amount that was left told people how much time had gone by. This clock did not rely on the sun, so it could be used at night.

Around A.D. 900, people began using candle clocks. A candle clock was a candle with marks on it. When the candle burned down to a mark, this showed that a certain amount of time had passed.

The sandglass was first used in the 1300s. It had a shape like the number 8. Sand was placed in the top part and ran through to the bottom. When all the sand had gone through, a certain amount of time had passed.

The first real clocks were very large and did not keep time very well. Later, clocks were made using springs. They were smaller and kept better time.

In the 1920s, quartz crystals were used in clocks. These clocks had no gears to wind or break. Most clocks today are made with quartz crystals.

Name _____ Date_____

1. Which idea should be included in a summary of this passage?

Ⓐ Sundials used the sun to tell time.

Ⓑ The sundial was invented long ago.

Ⓒ Sand was placed in the top part.

Ⓓ A candle clock was just a candle.

2. Which sentence best paraphrases the first two sentences in paragraph four?

Ⓐ When all the sand has gone through, a certain amount of time has passed.

Ⓑ Quartz crystals are very precise.

Ⓒ In the 1300s, people began to use a timepiece shaped like the number 8.

Ⓓ Clocks today have no gears to wind or break.

3. Which idea does NOT belong in a summary of this passage?

Ⓐ A candle burning down showed the passing of time.

Ⓑ Early clocks were large and did not keep time well.

Ⓒ In the sandglass, sand running through the glass marked an amount of time.

Ⓓ The water clock had sloping sides.

4. Write a summary of the first four paragraphs.

_____

_____

5. Write a summary of the last two paragraphs.

_____

_____

Name_____ Date _____

Directions: Read the passage. Then use the information from the passage to answer questions 1–5.

Circus Smirkus

Have you ever wanted to join the circus? Well, you can—at least for the summer.

Circus Smirkus is a circus for young people ages 10 to 20. You can try out for the circus. You can learn to juggle, walk on a wire, tumble, or be a clown. If you are good enough, you can spend the summer traveling with the circus.

Circus Smirkus was founded in the small town of Greensboro, Vermont. Young people from all over the world join the circus each year. Some even go to the Circus Camp in Craftsbury Common, Vermont. For one or two weeks, they learn circus skills. The best performers join the traveling circus group for the Summer Big Top Tour. Kids in this group train in June, after school has ended. Then they travel around New England and New York in July and August.

The Big Top Tour goes to 15 places each year. It gives 72 shows. Kids in the group help with all the work. They even set up the tent and sell tickets. Most of the money from ticket sales goes to support local programs, such as day-care centers and museums.

Joining Circus Smirkus is a great way to learn circus skills—and have a lot of fun!

Important Dates in Circus Smirkus History

1987: Circus Smirkus is founded by Rob Mermin, a circus clown.

1988: Circus Smirkus holds first Summer Big Top Tour.

1993: Summer Big Top Tour includes guests from Russia and ten Native American groups.

1997: Summer Tour plays 60 shows in New England.

2000: Circus Smirkus TV series is shown on Disney Channel.

2005: Smirkus School of Circus Arts opens in Essex, VT.

Name _____ Date_____

1. In what year was Circus Smirkus started?

Ⓐ 1987

Ⓑ 1988

Ⓒ 1999

Ⓓ 2001

2. What did Circus Smirkus do for the first time in 1988?

Ⓐ It was founded by Rob Mermin.

Ⓑ It included Native American performers.

Ⓒ It held a Summer Big Top Tour.

Ⓓ It opened a school of circus arts.

3. In what year did Circus Smirkus appear in a TV series?

Ⓐ 1987

Ⓑ 1993

Ⓒ 1997

Ⓓ 2000

4. What happened to Circus Smirkus in 2005?

_____

_____

5. Write two or three sentences describing the Summer Big Top Tour.

_____

_____

Name _____ Date _____

Directions: Read the passage. Then use the information from the passage to answer questions 1–5.

Homemade Homes

In the United States, most of the materials used to build homes are made in factories and mills. However, there are other kinds of homes. All around the world, people build homes from natural materials. Here are some examples.

Adobe house

This is a brick house. The bricks are made of adobe, which is a mixture of soil, clay, straw, and water. The bricks are dried in the sun. The roof of the house is made from wooden poles covered with brush and more adobe. Adobe houses are widely used in Mexico, the southwestern United States, and northern Africa.

Bedouin tent

This tent is made from woven goat hair. The roof is stretched over rows of wooden poles. The tent may be left open, or side cloths may be hung from the roof. Bedouin tents are used mainly in the deserts of Africa and Asia.

Yurt

This round house has a dome-shaped roof and walls made from pieces of wood tied together. Roof poles are placed on top of these walls. The house is covered with thick felt made from sheep's wool. Yurts are used in the wide open plains of Russia and Mongolia.

Name _____ Date_____

1. **You can tell from the descriptions that all three kinds of homes are built with _____.**

  Ⓐ clay   Ⓑ wood

  Ⓒ wool   Ⓓ grass

2. **Which kind of home has a flat roof?**

  Ⓐ tropical house   Ⓑ Bedouin tent

  Ⓒ adobe house   Ⓓ yurt

3. **Which kind of home does not have walls?**

  Ⓐ tropical house   Ⓑ Bedouin tent

  Ⓒ adobe house   Ⓓ yurt

4. **Name one or two ways in which the yurt and the Bedouin tent look similar.**

  _____

  _____

5. **How are most homes in the United States different from the homes shown in the pictures?**

  _____

  _____

Name _____ Date _____

Directions: Read the passage. Then use the information from the passage to answer questions 1–5.

Traveling Plants

Like many things in nature, "traveling" plants seem almost magical. But once you learn how these plants reproduce and grow, the magic will make sense.

Flowering plants produce seeds. Seeds are baby plants. These seeds are carried here and there in different ways.

Wind Some plant seeds are light and feathery. They can be carried a long way by the wind. The seeds of dandelions, milkweed, and maple trees are examples.

Dandelion and maple seeds travel on the wind.

Animals and People Other plant seeds stick to animal fur or people's clothes. Then they are carried to new places. These plants include plantain, burdock, and Queen Anne's lace.

Water Some plants drop their seeds into water. Then the seeds float away. The water lily and the coconut tree spread their seeds in this way. Unlike most seeds, the seeds from a coconut tree can live in salt water.

The leaves of water lilies are covered with jelly cases, which hold seeds. When the cases float away, the jelly melts, releasing the seeds.

Although seeds travel in different ways, the results are the same. When the seeds reach their new homes, some of them take root. These seeds grow into new plants. Then the new plants make more seeds.

Name _____ Date_____

1. Which kind of plant seed travels by wind?

Ⓐ coconut tree

Ⓑ Queen Anne's lace

Ⓒ maple tree

Ⓓ plantain

2. How do the seeds of water lilies travel?

Ⓐ They float by water.

Ⓑ They stick to animals.

Ⓒ They float through the air.

Ⓓ They stick to people's clothes.

3. How are all the seeds in the passage alike?

Ⓐ They all stick to animals.

Ⓑ They all grow in ponds.

Ⓒ They all travel.

Ⓓ They all float in the air.

4. How do jelly cases help seeds travel?

_____

_____

5. List three kinds of seeds that are carried by animals and people.

_____

_____

Name _____ Date _____

Directions: Read the passage. Then use the information from the passage to answer questions 1–5.

Use Your Beach Treasures

Do you like to find things on the beach? Do you pick up pretty shells and stones? Here are some ways to use and enjoy your beach treasures.

Sand *Make an outdoor sand lantern.** Open up a large paper bag. Fold the top down about six inches. Put five or six inches of sand in the bag. Place a candle in the sand. When it is dark, have a grown-up light the candle. Enjoy!

Pebbles *Make a pebble picture.* Collect a lot of interesting beach pebbles. Draw a picture on cardboard. Arrange pretty colored pebbles on the picture. Glue on the pebbles and let the glue dry overnight. Make a hole and hang your pebble picture with string. Enjoy!

Shells *Make some shell chimes.* Gather a lot of small shells with holes. Cut pieces of string about 12 inches long. Put one or more shells on each string. Tie knots to hold the shells in place. Now fasten all the strings to a stick or piece of wood. Hang your chimes by a window. Open the window so the wind rings the chimes. Enjoy!

Beach Glass *Make a beach glass ornament.* Find smooth, colored pieces of glass. Get a piece of clear plastic, such as a coffee can lid. Glue on the glass pieces. When the glue is dry, make a hole near one side. Hang your ornament with string. Hang it by a window so light comes through. Enjoy!

*A *lantern* is a kind of light or lamp.

Name _____ Date_____

1. What does the writer say to make from shells?

Ⓐ a picture   Ⓑ an ornament

Ⓒ chimes   Ⓓ a lantern

2. What part of the selection tells how to make a picture?

Ⓐ **Sand**   Ⓑ **Pebbles**

Ⓒ **Shells**   Ⓓ **Beach Glass**

3. Why should you hang a beach glass ornament near a window?

Ⓐ to be safe

Ⓑ so the wind can blow it

Ⓒ to help the glue dry

Ⓓ so light comes through

4. What is a *lantern*?

_____

_____

5. Name three kinds of beach treasures from this passage. Tell what you can do with each kind of treasure.

_____

_____

_____

_____

Name _____ Date _____

Directions: Read the passage. Then use the information from the passage to answer questions 1–5.

She Put Science Into Words

Rachel Carson was born in 1907. She grew up on a farm. Rachel loved to learn about nature. She also loved writing. Every month, she <u>received</u> a magazine in the mail. It had stories about young people. Rachel decided to send in one of her own stories. The magazine accepted it and gave Rachel a prize.

After college, Rachel went to work at the U.S. Bureau of Fisheries. She was a scientist. Her job was to write booklets and articles. In her free time, she also wrote her own books. They were about nature and science.

One of Rachel's interests was bug sprays. Poison sprays were widely used then to kill insects. No one knew how <u>dangerous</u> the sprays were to animals and people.

Rachel's book *Silent Spring* came out in 1963. It warned against the use of these sprays. It said they posed many dangers. Her book led to new laws to <u>govern</u> the use of poison sprays.

Rachel Carson died in 1964, not long after she finished *Silent Spring*. Today she is <u>remembered</u> as a fine science writer. She helped make the world a safer and better place.

Name _____ Date _____

1. The passage says, "Every month, she <u>received</u> a magazine."
   Which word means the *opposite* of <u>received</u>?
   Ⓐ got   Ⓑ sent
   Ⓒ wrote   Ⓓ took

2. The passage says that no one knew how <u>dangerous</u> the
   sprays could be. Which word has almost the same meaning
   as <u>dangerous</u>?
   Ⓐ useful   Ⓑ harmful
   Ⓒ important   Ⓓ expensive

3. In which sentence is the underlined word used correctly?
   Ⓐ *Silent Spring* was written <u>buy</u> Rachel Carson.
   Ⓑ We sat down <u>buy</u> the lake.
   Ⓒ I want to <u>buy</u> one of her books.
   Ⓓ She left her coat <u>buy</u> the door.

4. The passage says that *Silent Spring* "led to new laws to
   <u>govern</u> the use of poison sprays." Which word means about
   the same as <u>govern</u>?
   Ⓐ control   Ⓑ increase
   Ⓒ encourage   Ⓓ vote

5. The passage says, "Today she is <u>remembered</u> as a fine science
   writer." Which word means the *opposite* of <u>remembered</u>?
   Ⓐ recalled   Ⓑ admired
   Ⓒ viewed   Ⓓ forgotten

Name _____ Date _____

Directions: Read the passage. Then use the information from the passage to answer questions 1–5.

Today's Rodeo

Have you ever seen a rodeo? It can be an exciting show. It is also a contest for both men and women. <u>There</u> are several different events.

Some of the events come from things that cowboys do in their jobs. Calf roping is one event like that. A cowboy on a horse must rope a calf and tie it down as <u>swiftly</u> as he can. The record for this event is 6.9 seconds!

Some rodeo events are quite <u>risky</u>, such as bull riding and bronco riding. In these events, a cowboy rides a <u>wild</u> bull or a wild horse. He has no saddle or bridle. He holds onto a strap. The strap is tied around the animal's belly. The goal is to stay on the animal for as long as he can. When the rider falls off, a clown runs in to get the animal's attention. Otherwise, the animal might <u>injure</u> the rider.

Barrel racing is a skill event for a horse and rider. The cowboy or cowgirl rides the horse around three barrels placed in a triangle. It is a race against the clock.

Thousands of people enjoy rodeos every year.

Name _____ Date_____

1. In which sentence is the underlined word used correctly?

(A) <u>Their</u> is a rodeo next week.

(B) The cowboys wave to <u>there</u> friends.

(C) Uncle John is sitting over <u>their</u>.

(D) Cowboys take care of <u>their</u> horses.

2. The passage says, "A cowboy on a horse must rope a calf and tie it down as <u>swiftly</u> as he can." Which word means the *opposite* of <u>swiftly</u>?

(A) quickly   (B) calmly

(C) slowly   (D) nicely

3. "Some rodeo events are quite <u>risky</u>." Which word means about the same as <u>risky</u>?

(A) dangerous   (B) clever

(C) exciting   (D) funny

4. The passage says, "A cowboy rides a <u>wild</u> bull." Which word means the *opposite* of <u>wild</u>?

(A) fierce   (B) strong

(C) large   (D) tame

5. "The animal might <u>injure</u> the rider." Which word means the same as <u>injure</u>?

(A) help   (B) harm

(C) cover   (D) protect

Name ——————————————— Date ————————

Directions: Read the passage. Then use the information from the passage to answer questions 1–5.

Crickets

Crickets are known <u>primarily</u> for their chirping. People in many parts of the world know the sound crickets make.

Crickets have two pairs of wings. Male crickets make noise by rubbing their front wings together. They do this to <u>attract</u> female crickets. The females hear sounds through their legs.

Females listen to the chirping sound and use it to <u>locate</u> the males. The females hop toward the sound. Their powerful back legs <u>enable</u> them to travel quickly. A cricket can go two feet in one jump with these legs.

A cricket chirps faster as the temperature goes up. You can <u>calculate</u> the temperature outside by listening to a cricket! Count the number of chirps one cricket makes in 15 seconds. Then add 40 to this number. The sum is the temperature!

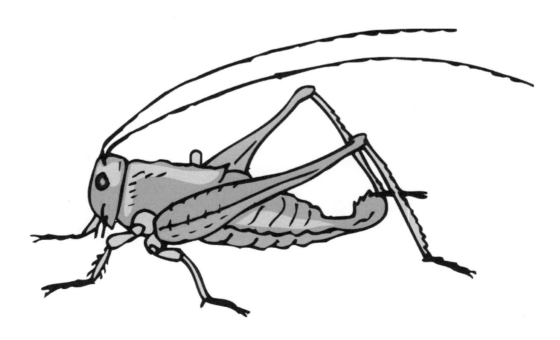

Name _____ Date_____

1. The passage says, "Crickets are known <u>primarily</u> for their chirping." What does <u>primarily</u> mean?

Ⓐ loudly   Ⓑ never

Ⓒ sadly   Ⓓ mostly

2. "They do this to <u>attract</u> female crickets." The word <u>attract</u> means _____.

Ⓐ get the attention of   Ⓑ gather food for

Ⓒ jump in the direction of   Ⓓ scare away

3. The passage says, "Their powerful back legs <u>enable</u> them to travel quickly." The word <u>enable</u> means _____.

Ⓐ allow   Ⓑ hide

Ⓒ force   Ⓓ tell

4. "Females listen to the chirping sound and use it to <u>locate</u> the males." What words in the passage help you know that <u>locate</u> means "to find"?

_____

_____

5. "You can <u>calculate</u> the temperature outside by listening to a cricket!" What clues in the passage help you know that <u>calculate</u> means "figure out"?

_____

_____

Name————————————————— Date —————————

Directions: Read the passage. Then use the information from the passage to answer questions 1–5.

Crossing the Country

In 1903, very few Americans had cars. Most people traveled by horse. The country had only 150 miles of paved roads. There were no highways or road maps. There were no gas stations. These were <u>major</u> problems. But they did not stop Horatio Nelson Jackson. Dr. Jackson wanted to drive across the United States. So that is what he did.

Horatio Jackson's trip <u>commenced</u> in San Francisco, California. He packed his 1903 Winton car with spare parts. He also took camping gear. Then he named his car the *Vermont*. Jackson and his wife Bertha came from Vermont <u>originally</u>. They had traveled all over North America by train and horse. Now they were going home.

Jackson left California on May 23. He arrived in New York City 63 days later. In many places he visited along the way, people had never seen a car. In one town, he ran out of gas. His car had to be <u>towed</u> to the next ranch by a cowboy on a horse. Sometimes Jackson needed spare parts for his car. He ordered them by telegraph. Days later, the parts came by <u>stagecoach</u>. The coach was pulled by horses.

Jackson's car broke down many times. He replaced the tires many times, too. But he made the trip. He also won a $50 bet. His friends had bet that he would never make it to New York in a car.

Name _____ Date_____

1. The passage says, "These were <u>major</u> problems." What does <u>major</u> mean?
   Ⓐ funny
   Ⓑ costly
   Ⓒ big
   Ⓓ extra

2. The passage says, "His car had to be <u>towed</u> to the next ranch by a cowboy on a horse." The word <u>towed</u> means _____.
   Ⓐ sold
   Ⓑ led
   Ⓒ pulled
   Ⓓ oiled

3. "Days later, the parts came by <u>stagecoach</u>." What is a <u>stagecoach</u>?
   Ⓐ a small truck with four wheels
   Ⓑ a kind of wagon pulled by horses
   Ⓒ a train powered by steam
   Ⓓ a team of riders working together

4. "Horatio Jackson's trip <u>commenced</u> in San Francisco." What words in the passage tell you that <u>commenced</u> means "started"?

   _____

   _____

5. "Jackson and his wife Bertha came from Vermont <u>originally</u>." What clues in the passage tell you that <u>originally</u> means "at first"?

   _____

   _____

Name _____ Date _____

Directions: Read the passage. Then use the information from the passage to answer questions 1–5.

Everyday Inventions

Some inventions have changed the world in big ways. Others have <u>reformed</u> the world in small ways. But they are still important. Think about these examples.

What would life be like without soap? Soap was first made about 2,000 years ago. <u>Previously</u>, one way to clean clothes was to pound them on rocks by a stream.

Can you imagine writing with a feather? Long ago, people used the quill of a feather. They dipped it in ink and used it to write. In the 1800s, people began to use metal pen points. In 1884, Lewis Waterman made the first pen that held its own ink!

Today, millions of people use zippers. They are used on jackets and coats, pants, dresses, and boots. A man named Whitcomb Judson invented the zipper in 1891. Before that, most clothes were <u>fastened</u> with buttons.

Before 1909, people <u>must've</u> made toast by holding bread over an open fire. Then the first electric toaster came out. But it toasted only one side of the bread. If the plug wasn't pulled as soon as the toast was done, the bread burned. After many years, an <u>inventor</u> made a new toaster. It turned itself off when the toast was done.

Comprehension Strategy Assessment • Grade 3

Name _____ Date_____

1. The passage says, "Others have <u>reformed</u> the world in small ways." What does the word <u>reformed</u> mean?

Ⓐ colored   Ⓑ moved

Ⓒ changed   Ⓓ quieted

2. "<u>Previously</u>, one way to clean clothes was to pound them on rocks by a stream." The word <u>previously</u> means _____.

Ⓐ before that   Ⓑ during that time

Ⓒ after that   Ⓓ instead of that

3. "Most clothes were <u>fastened</u> with buttons." What does <u>fastened</u> mean?

Ⓐ colored   Ⓑ moved faster

Ⓒ sold   Ⓓ held together

4. The passage says, "People <u>must've</u> made toast." What does <u>must've</u> mean?

Ⓐ must give   Ⓑ must have

Ⓒ must live   Ⓓ must love

5. "An <u>inventor</u> made a new toaster." An <u>inventor</u> is a _____.

Ⓐ place   Ⓑ new tool

Ⓒ person   Ⓓ kind of bread

Name _____ Date _____

Directions: *Read the passage. Then use the information from the passage to answer questions 1–5.*

The Little Giant

This man is called the "Little Giant." But he sure isn't little. Yao Ming is 7 feet 6 inches tall! He weighs 310 pounds. Yao Ming plays for the Houston Rockets basketball team. He scores an average of more than 18 points per game.

Yao Ming was born in China. Both of his parents were tall and played basketball. Ming played for the Shanghai Sharks in China. With his <u>assistance</u>, the Sharks won the championship.

In 2000, Yao Ming played for China in the Summer Olympics. Many coaches from the NBA saw him play. Two years later, he was picked to play for the Houston Rockets. When he got to Houston, he could not speak English. He needed a <u>translator</u> to help him.

Since his first season in Houston, Yao has become very popular with fans. He is friendly and <u>likable</u>. He was <u>chosen</u> to play on the NBA All-Star Team. In his free time, Yao helps to raise money to fight SARS. SARS is a disease that was first <u>discovered</u> in China.

Name _____ Date_____

1. The passage says, "With his <u>assistance</u>, the Sharks won the championship." What does the word <u>assistance</u> mean?

(A) name

(B) height

(C) help

(D) family

2. "He needed a <u>translator</u> to help him." You can tell from the word that a <u>translator</u> is a _____.

(A) person

(B) machine

(C) tool

(D) book

3. The passage says, "He is friendly and <u>likable</u>." The word <u>likable</u> means that he _____.

(A) likes everyone

(B) is not well liked

(C) likes to play basketball

(D) is easy to like

4. "He was <u>chosen</u> to play on the NBA All-Star Team." The word <u>chosen</u> means _____.

(A) too tall

(B) picked

(C) not ready

(D) paid

5. The passage says that SARS "was first <u>discovered</u> in China." The word <u>discovered</u> means _____.

(A) covered again

(B) cured

(C) covered well

(D) found

Posttest

Answer Key

1. D	17. A
2. C	18. D
3. B	19. A
4. A	20. C
5. A	21. C
6. D	22. B
7. C	23. C
8. B	24. A
9. D	25. A
10. B	26. B
11. A	27. D
12. D	28. B
13. B	29. C
14. D	30. C
15. B	31. A
16. C	32. B

Name _____ Date _____

Directions: Read the passage. Then use the information from the passage to answer questions 1–4.

The Coyote and the Rabbit

Long ago, a rabbit and a coyote lived in the forest. The coyote liked the rabbit. He thought Rabbit was his friend. But Rabbit did not think much of Coyote. Mostly she had fun playing tricks on him.

One day, Rabbit was sitting beside a pond. She saw Coyote coming her way. When Coyote drew near, Rabbit said, "I am glad to see you! I need your help."

"There is a big cheese at the bottom of the pond," said Rabbit. "We can get the cheese by drinking the pond dry."

Coyote looked. He saw only a large white rock. He began drinking the pond water in big gulps.

After a minute, Rabbit hopped off. "I'm going to look for more help," she called. "I'll be back soon." But she never returned.

In the meantime, Coyote kept gulping down the pond water. His belly grew full and <u>tight</u>. Then it began to ache. Many hours passed before the ache went away.

Name _____ Date_____

1. Which words best describe the character of Coyote in this story?

Ⓐ mean and tricky

Ⓑ careful and wise

Ⓒ strong and brave

Ⓓ foolish and trusting

2. In this story, what is Coyote's main problem?

Ⓐ He does not like Rabbit.

Ⓑ He is very thirsty.

Ⓒ He believes what Rabbit says.

Ⓓ He is hungry for cheese.

3. Which sentence tells something that could happen in real life?

Ⓐ The coyote thinks the rabbit is his friend.

Ⓑ The rabbit sees the coyote coming her way.

Ⓒ The rabbit asks the coyote for help.

Ⓓ The coyote drinks all the water out of a pond.

4. The story says, "His belly grew full and <u>tight</u>." Which word means the *opposite* of <u>tight</u>?

Ⓐ loose

Ⓑ strong

Ⓒ empty

Ⓓ sore

Name _____ Date_____

Directions: Read the passage. Then use the information from the passage to answer questions 5–8.

The Treasure of Range Creek Canyon

About 60 years ago, a young cowboy found an important treasure. The cowboy's name was Waldo Wilcox. The treasure was a grass basket in a stone house. What made the basket and house important? They were made by the Fremont Indians. These Indians lived more than 1,000 years ago.

Wilcox found the treasure in Range Creek Canyon in Utah. Range Creek Canyon is a wild place, far from roads or big towns. Wilcox found other treasures there, too. He found bits of pottery. He found tools and beads. He also found many more stone houses.

Wilcox could have gathered up the treasures. He could have sold them for a lot of money. But he did not. Wilcox wanted the treasures to stay just as the Indians had left them. So Wilcox bought the land where he found the treasures. He built gates to keep people out. Only his wife and children knew his secret.

A few years ago, Wilcox decided to sell his land. But he wanted to make sure the treasures would be <u>preserved</u>. So Wilcox sold the land to the U.S. government. Now experts can visit the land. They can examine the treasures. Before long, they will tell the rest of the world what they have learned about the Fremont Indians. This makes Waldo Wilcox feel proud.

5. What is the main idea of this passage?

Ⓐ Waldo Wilcox found an important treasure in Range Creek Canyon.

Ⓑ Range Creek Canyon is far from roads or big towns.

Ⓒ Waldo Wilcox shared a secret with his wife and children.

Ⓓ Now the government owns the land in Range Creek Canyon.

6. Which detail shows that the things Wilcox found were important?

Ⓐ The treasure was a grass basket in a stone house.

Ⓑ Range Creek Canyon is in Utah.

Ⓒ Wilcox also found pottery, tools, and beads.

Ⓓ He could have sold the treasure for a lot of money.

7. The passage says, "He wanted to make sure the treasures would be preserved." What does preserved mean?

Ⓐ taken away   Ⓑ used

Ⓒ kept safe   Ⓓ sold

8. The author wrote this passage to _____.

Ⓐ describe what Range Creek Canyon looks like

Ⓑ give information about Waldo Wilcox and his treasure

Ⓒ tell a funny story about a cowboy named Waldo

Ⓓ explain why the Fremont Indians lived in Range Creek Canyon

Name_____ Date _____

Directions: Read the passage. Then use the information from the passage to answer questions 9–12.

Gita's New Job

"Boys and girls, it's the first day of a new month," said Ms. Mayo. "That means it's time to change class jobs. Please look at the job chart to find your new job."

Gita smiled when she found her name. Finally, she was the pet feeder! She <u>peered</u> at Danny and Donny. The two brown gerbils turned toward Gita. Danny, the slim one, was quiet. But his chubby brother squeaked loudly.

Gita gave the gerbils fresh water. Then she poured food into the empty dish.

Brrrriiiiiiiinnnggggggg! The fire bell made Gita jump. "Everyone stop what you're doing and line up," said Ms. Mayo. Then she led her class down the hall and outside.

When the fire drill ended, Ms. Mayo's class returned to their room. Something small and brown raced across the floor. Everyone but Gita laughed and squealed. She picked up the gerbil. Feeling its slim body in her hands, Gita said, "Back to your cage, Danny."

When Gita reached the cage, its door was wide open. But Donny was still inside eating. He had missed his chance to get out.

9. What will Gita do next?

Ⓐ   She will get another job.

Ⓑ   She will take Donny out of the cage.

Ⓒ   She will put more food in the dish.

Ⓓ   She will put Danny back in the cage.

10. What happens in this story after Gita gets a new job?

Ⓐ   Ms. Mayo's class gets two new gerbils.

Ⓑ   The class has a fire drill.

Ⓒ   Ms. Mayo's class has snack time.

Ⓓ   The class gets a new teacher.

11. How did Danny get out of the cage?

Ⓐ   Gita left the cage door open.

Ⓑ   Ms. Mayo let Danny out.

Ⓒ   Danny broke open the cage door.

Ⓓ   One of Gita's classmates let Danny out.

**12. The story says, "She <u>peered</u> at Danny and Donny."
What does <u>peered</u> mean?**

Ⓐ   laughed

Ⓑ   talked loudly

Ⓒ   pushed

Ⓓ   looked closely

Name _____ Date _____

Directions: Read the passage. Then use the information from the passage to answer questions 13–17.

An Artist by Chance

Grandma Moses is a famous American painter. But she never planned to be a painter. She never dreamed of being famous, either. All this happened to Grandma Moses by chance.

Grandma Moses' real name was Anna Mary Robertson. She was born in 1860 in New York State. She was raised on a farm. When she grew up, she married a farmer named Thomas Moses. As a farm wife, Anna Moses worked hard. But she liked to make pretty needlework pictures in her free time.

Grandma Moses started painting when she was nearly 70 years old. Her hands had <u>stiffened</u> with age. She had to give up her needlework. So she took up painting. She painted charming scenes of country life.

One day in 1938, a man named Louis Caldor stopped in the town where Grandma Moses lived. Mr. Caldor knew a lot about art. He saw some of Grandma Moses' paintings in a shop window. He bought the paintings. He put them in an art show in New York City. The show made Grandma Moses famous!

Grandma Moses died in 1961. She lived to be 101. But she never had to give up painting. In the last year of her life, she painted 25 pictures.

13. Most of the information in the passage is organized by _____.

Ⓐ cause and effect   Ⓑ time order

Ⓒ compare and contrast   Ⓓ order of importance

14. Why did Louis Caldor buy Grandma Moses' paintings?

Ⓐ They did not cost much.

Ⓑ He wanted to remember his trip to New York.

Ⓒ Grandma Moses needed the money.

Ⓓ He thought Grandma Moses was a great painter.

15. Which sentence states an opinion?

Ⓐ Grandma Moses started painting when she was nearly 70.

Ⓑ Her paintings were charming.

Ⓒ Louis Caldor saw her paintings in a shop.

Ⓓ He put them in an art show in New York.

16. The passage says, "Her hands had <u>stiffened</u> with age." What does <u>stiffened</u> mean?

Ⓐ gained a special skill   Ⓑ turned a different color

Ⓒ became difficult to move or use   Ⓓ got covered with paint

17. The author wrote this passage to _____.

Ⓐ tell how Grandma Moses became a painter

Ⓑ make readers want to try painting

Ⓒ compare Grandma Moses with other painters

Ⓓ tell why people should buy paintings

Name _____ Date _____

Directions: Read the passage. Then use the information from the passage to answer questions 18–22.

Your Body's Fuel

"I'm running out of gas." You've probably heard a hungry person say this. It's true that your body is a bit like a car. You need fuel to run. When you're low on fuel, you can't work or play like you should.

Have you ever watched someone putting gas in a car? When the car's tank is full, the gas shuts off. There's no way to put too much gas in a car. But it's not the same for you. You can eat enough food to <u>refuel</u> your body. If you eat more food than your body needs, you will put on some extra pounds.

> ## Say no to soda!
>
> Thirsty? Don't reach for soda pop! A can of soda has about 150 calories. Those calories can add up to extra pounds if you're not careful. Drinking water is a smarter move. No matter how much you drink, water has NO calories.

Doctors use calories to measure how much food energy you should take in each day. Most kids need about 2,200 calories a day. But the number is higher if you exercise.

What kinds of exercise burn the most calories? Take a look at the graph to find out.

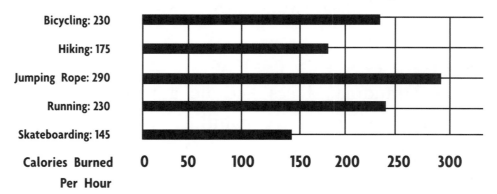

Calories Burned While Exercising

Exercise	Calories Burned Per Hour
Bicycling: 230	
Hiking: 175	
Jumping Rope: 290	
Running: 230	
Skateboarding: 145	

Calories Burned Per Hour: 0   50   100   150   200   250   300

18. The passage says, "You can eat enough food to <u>refuel</u> your body." What does <u>refuel</u> mean?

Ⓐ like fuel   Ⓑ not fuel

Ⓒ without fuel   Ⓓ fuel again

19. Which is the best summary of the first paragraph?

Ⓐ Your body is like a car because both need fuel.

Ⓑ Hungry people often say, "I'm running out of gas."

Ⓒ Cars and people don't need that much fuel.

Ⓓ There are some funny ways to say, "I'm hungry."

20. How many calories does a can of soda have?

Ⓐ 2,200   Ⓑ 200

Ⓒ 150   Ⓓ 0

21. Which kind of exercise burns the fewest calories in an hour?

Ⓐ jumping rope   Ⓑ bicycling

Ⓒ skateboarding   Ⓓ running

22. About how many calories will you burn if you hike for an hour?

Ⓐ 150   Ⓑ 175

Ⓒ 230   Ⓓ 290

Name _____ Date _____

Directions: Read the passage. Then use the information from the passage to answer questions 23–27.

Stella's Journal

July 6

Great news! Mom and Dad will let Ruby and me sleep outside on Friday night. We're going to borrow a tent and sleeping bags from Uncle Pete. I can hardly wait!

July 7

Ruby has been teasing me about our sleep-out. She says I'm going to get scared and run inside. Just because she's older, she thinks she's so <u>mature</u> and brave. I'm not worried, though. We're just going to be in the backyard. How scary can that be?

July 8

Here we are! Ruby and I are inside the tent. It got dark an hour ago. That's when we came out and tucked ourselves into our sleeping bags. We've been reading books and talking. This is so much fun! I'll bet Ruby is surprised that —

July 9

Oh, boy! I never got to finish that last sentence. As I was writing, something brushed up against the outside of our tent. It was big, and it was panting loudly. Ruby whispered, "Maybe it's a wolf." That's all I needed to hear. I ran to the back door and pounded on it until Mom let me in. I didn't go back out.

When Ruby came in for breakfast this morning, she was laughing. She said that after I ran inside, Scruffy wandered into the tent. He curled up on my sleeping bag and fell asleep.

23. What can you conclude from this story?

Ⓐ Uncle Pete tried to scare the girls.

Ⓑ A wolf sneaked into the tent.

Ⓒ Scruffy is the family's dog.

Ⓓ Stella is older than Ruby.

24. How is Stella different from Ruby?

Ⓐ Stella did not stay outside all night.

Ⓑ Stella had to borrow a sleeping bag.

Ⓒ Stella read books inside the tent.

Ⓓ Stella did not hear anything outside the tent.

25. Which of these events happened first?

Ⓐ Ruby and Stella borrowed a tent.

Ⓑ Stella pounded on the back door.

Ⓒ The girls climbed into their sleeping bags.

Ⓓ Stella and Ruby got into the tent.

26. Stella ran out of the tent because _____.

Ⓐ Mom was calling her   Ⓑ she thought she heard a wolf

Ⓒ Ruby was keeping her awake Ⓓ she wanted to find Scruffy

27. The passage says, "Just because she's older, she thinks she's so <u>mature</u> and brave." What does <u>mature</u> mean?

Ⓐ bossy   Ⓑ important

Ⓒ smart   Ⓓ grown–up

Name ———————————————————— Date ——————

Directions: Read the passage. Then use the information from the passage to answer questions 28–32.

Two Pilots

On May 20, 1927, a plane took off from Long Island, New York. It flew east over the Atlantic Ocean. The next day the plane landed in Paris, France. The pilot was Charles Lindbergh. He stepped from the plane. A huge crowd cheered for him. Lindbergh was the first person to fly alone across the Atlantic without stopping. The trip took about 33 hours.

Almost 80 years later, a man named Steve Fossett became "the new Lindbergh." He was even more daring than Lindbergh. Fossett's trip began on February 28, 2005. His plane <u>departed</u> from Salina, Kansas. Like Lindbergh, Fossett flew east and crossed the Atlantic. But his trip did not end there. Fossett kept on flying east. He flew across Africa. Then he flew across Asia. He flew across the Pacific Ocean, too.

On March 3, Fossett returned to Salina, Kansas. He was the first person to fly alone around the world nonstop. His trip lasted 67 hours. It was twice as long as Lindbergh's trip.

28. How were Lindbergh and Fossett's trips alike?

Ⓐ Both flew over Asia and Africa.

Ⓑ Both flew alone on their trips.

Ⓒ Both took off from Long Island.

Ⓓ Both stopped during their trips.

29. Which sentence from the passage states an opinion?

Ⓐ A huge crowd cheered for him.

Ⓑ Lindbergh was the first person to fly alone across the Atlantic.

Ⓒ He was even more daring than Lindbergh.

Ⓓ It was twice as long as Lindbergh's trip.

30. The passage says, "His plane <u>departed</u> from Salina, Kansas." What does <u>departed</u> mean?

Ⓐ fell   Ⓑ remained

Ⓒ left   Ⓓ followed

31. Both Lindbergh and Fossett were <u>daring</u> men. Which word means the same as <u>daring</u>?

Ⓐ brave   Ⓑ strong

Ⓒ foolish   Ⓓ lonely

32. Which is the best summary of this passage?

Ⓐ Charles Lindbergh and Steve Fossett took long plane trips. Fossett's trip took twice as long as Lindbergh's.

Ⓑ In 1927, Charles Lindbergh became the first person to fly alone across the Atlantic. In 2005, Steve Fossett became the first person to fly alone around the world.

Ⓒ Many people cheered when Charles Lindbergh landed his plane in Paris. But Steve Fossett flew around the world without stopping.

Ⓓ These days, planes can fly a long way without stopping. Steve Fossett flew his plane all around the world in 67 hours.

Answer Sheet

Student Name _____ Date _____

Teacher Name _____ Grade _____

Pretest Posttest
(Circle one.)

1. (A) (B) (C) (D)   17. (A) (B) (C) (D)
2. (A) (B) (C) (D)   18. (A) (B) (C) (D)
3. (A) (B) (C) (D)   19. (A) (B) (C) (D)
4. (A) (B) (C) (D)   20. (A) (B) (C) (D)
5. (A) (B) (C) (D)   21. (A) (B) (C) (D)
6. (A) (B) (C) (D)   22. (A) (B) (C) (D)
7. (A) (B) (C) (D)   23. (A) (B) (C) (D)
8. (A) (B) (C) (D)   24. (A) (B) (C) (D)
9. (A) (B) (C) (D)   25. (A) (B) (C) (D)
10. (A) (B) (C) (D)   26. (A) (B) (C) (D)
11. (A) (B) (C) (D)   27. (A) (B) (C) (D)
12. (A) (B) (C) (D)   28. (A) (B) (C) (D)
13. (A) (B) (C) (D)   29. (A) (B) (C) (D)
14. (A) (B) (C) (D)   30. (A) (B) (C) (D)
15. (A) (B) (C) (D)   31. (A) (B) (C) (D)
16. (A) (B) (C) (D)   32. (A) (B) (C) (D)

Student Name _____ Date _____

Teacher Name _____ Grade _____

Tested Skills

Cluster Comprehension and Word Solving Skills	Item Numbers				Pretest Score	Posttest Score
1 Literary Elements Analyze Character Analyze Story Elements Distinguish Real from Make-Believe	1	2	3	10	/4	/4
2 Text Structure and Features Analyze Text Structure and Organization Use Graphic Features to Interpret Information Use Text Features to Locate Information	13	20	21	22	/4	/4
3 Relating Ideas Compare and Contrast Identify Cause and Effect Identify Sequence or Steps in a Process	24	25	26	28	/4	/4
4 Inferences and Conclusions Draw Conclusions Make Inferences Make Predictions	9	11	14	23	/4	/4
5 Making Judgments Evaluate Author's Purpose and Point of View Distinguish Fact from Opinion	8	15	17	29	/4	/4
6 Distinguishing Important Information Identify Main Idea and Supporting Details Summarize or Paraphrase Information	5	6	19	32	/4	/4
7 Context Clues Use context clues to determine word meaning	7	12	16	27	/4	/4
8 Word Families and Structures Identify synonyms, antonyms, and homonyms Use knowledge of word structure to determine word meaning	4	18	30	31	/4	/4
	Total				/32	/32

Pretest Score		Posttest Score	
Number Correct/Total	Percent Score	Number Correct/Total	Percent Score
/32	%	/32	%

Teacher Name ——————————————————————— Grade ——————————

Student Name	Pretest		Posttest		Comparison/ Notes
	Total No. Correct	Percent Score	Total No. Correct	Percent Score	

Student Name _____

Teacher Name _____ Grade _____

Assessments	Comprehension/ Word Solving Skills	Reading or Listening		Reading or Listening	
		Date of 1st Assessment	Score	Date of 2nd Assessment	Score
1–2	Analyze Character				
3–4	Analyze Story Elements				
5–6	Analyze Text Structure and Organization				
7–8	Compare and Contrast				
9–10	Distinguish Fact from Opinion				
11–12	Distinguish Real from Make-Believe				
13–14	Draw Conclusions				
15–16	Evaluate Author's Purpose and Point of View				
17–18	Identify Cause and Effect				
19–20	Identify Main Idea and Supporting Details				
21–22	Identify Sequence or Steps in a Process				
23–24	Make Inferences				
25–26	Make Predictions				
27–28	Summarize or Paraphrase Information				
29–30	Use Graphic Features to Interpret Information				
31–32	Use Text Features to Locate Information				
33–34	Identify Synonyms, Antonyms, and Homonyms				
35–36	Use Context Clues to Determine Word Meaning				
37–38	Use Knowledge of Word Structure to Determine Word Meaning				

Comprehension Strategy Assessment • Grade 3

Comprehension Strategy Assessment • Grade 3   © 2006 Benchmark Education Company, LLC